Blood Moo

C000114536

By Paul Lunel

Dedication

This novel is dedicated to my fantastic wife, Lucie who challenged me to write, and said I would not see it through, and also my Mom (RIP). Both of them were and are an amazing support team. I Love them both.

Acknowledgements

The Lord Above for blessing me with the gift to put my imagination on paper.

Lucie and Mom. Both were used as soundboards, both of them ended up proof reading more than once, and the hours that Lucie put in going over the manuscript...doing her best to edit...never been there before.

Full credit for the awesome cover goes to The Book Khaleesi and I would like to Thank and Acknowledge Eeva as the illustrator on Amazon. Find this amazing lady @ www.thebookkhaleesi.com

Prologue

A full moon looks down on the dry African bush. The wind plays with the leaves of the trees. Shadows grow longer as the moon climbs in the sky. A Howl reverberates across the vast African landscape, splitting the night in two freezing the leopard in his tracks. He moves from the safety of the shrubs. Silence descends like a blanket. The chirping of the crickets and the mating call of the frogs disappear as the haunting cry rings off the kopje behind the big cat.

Shadows hide the other as it watches as the spotted feline moves slowly around the corner of the deserted house. The attack is fast and deadly. The watcher launches itself onto the back of the cat, its strong jaws latching onto the thick neck of the leopard, just behind the head.

Rolling onto its back the spitting cat tries to dislodge its attacker, blood flies. Bone is crushed and the spinal cord severed, the big cat now paralyzed is at the mercy of the creature of the night. The head of the leopard is torn from its body; sounds of ripping and tearing now fill the night as the other eats.

An abomination stands in the clearing; all is still, Africa waits; it lifts its head to the heavens and howls out its ownership of the night.

Nothing is safe when the moon is full.

Sun rises on a new morning, the area behind the house is deserted, the scene of the battle and the spoor in the dirt tells a story of its own, leopard spoor cover's the area and covering the leopard spoor are tracks of another.

Dried blood splatter marks the walls of the house, and the torn decapitated body of the leopard, half eaten lies in the dirt.

Mother Nature uses the wind to slowly sweep the area clean, and soon there is nothing to tell the story the slate has been wiped clean. Nature will take care of the rest.

Glassy dead eyes of the leopard look out from its detached head, on the rubbish dump.

Thick bush surrounds the house that stands alone at the end of a long rutted overgrown dirt track. Inside the house the dust on the floor is thick, cobwebs fill the corners, and the bath is full of bits and pieces that have built up over the years. The stable door leading from the kitchen into the back area hangs on it rusted hinges, broken.

There are no birds nesting in the house, it's free of mice and rats and the only thing that shows that any living thing was there are the prints in the dust.

Chapter 1

With a screech and the smell of burning rubber the large wheels of the 747 touches down on runway 26 at Lusaka International Airport. David turns to his new bride a bright bubbly 27-year-old blonde with large brown eyes and smiles. "Welcome to Africa my darling."

Adele's eyes are alive with wonder as she looks out the window as the big jet lands, excitement running through her veins, a new chapter has opened in her life and she is now in Africa to share that chapter with the man she loves. The man who is gentle, caring and most important who loves her with every ounce of his being. She feels safe with David and it did not take her long to say yes to his proposal of marriage, nor to the move from her home in London, to live in the wilds of Africa.

Excited but weary passengers disembark and move across the tarmac to the terminal building, moving through customs and into the reception area. "David" a voice bellows across the open space.

A larger than life specimen of a man pushes his way through the crowd dressed all in khaki takes David into a bear hug, both men are in their late thirty's and grew up together. "Man it's good to see you again, this must be Mrs. Swart, hell David, she is far too *lekker* for you." With a smile, David turns to his blushing bride.

"Adele, I would like you to meet Piet Van Zyl, he's the local hunter in these parts and my best friend."

"Best friend *se voët*, I never even got an invite to the bloody wedding; good thing though as I would have convinced Adele to run away with me." He offers Adele his hand, the size of a melon. "Welcome to Africa Mrs. Swart, follow me I have wheels outside. Let me take you to your hotel, and we can make arrangements to get you out to your home in the morning."

Piet drives through the traffic of central Lusaka, like a bull in a china shop, and finally, much to both David and Adele's relief, they arrive at the hotel, in one piece. "You two check in, and meet me on the veranda for a beer, I need to fill you in and bring you up to date on a few things David, things have changed over the last few years, and there's a lot to talk about."

As David and Adele return from checking in and cross the broad veranda towards the burly South Africa, Piet gets to his feet in greeting, a broad grin on his rugged features. "I took the liberty of ordering you a Beer Shandy Adele, that is half beer and half lemonade, and for you David, an ice cold Black Label with your name on it, Man it's great to see you again."

Helping Adele into a chair, David turns to his boyhood friend. "You're looking good Piet, and thanks for the beer, this is going to go down well." A serious look comes into the big man's eyes as he leans across the table towards the two. "Guys, you need to know that your house needs work. I mean a lot of work, so you'll be living in a tent for about three weeks and Adele, you will have to get used to using an outhouse until everything is up and running, that includes the generator, so no lights for a while but hey man this is Africa, you're in the bush miles from anyone, what more could you ask for?"

**

A full moon climbs slowly above the clouds as they run across the sky full and bright, throwing shadows on the ground. The area around the house is desolate; there is no evidence of bird life. Crickets start their concert, backed up by the sound of the frogs from the nearby Kafue River, the wind plays amongst the trees and the night waits.

Slowly a jackal leaves its den in a nearby outcrop and lifts its head to pay homage to the moon. She howls her greeting to the night and then moves across the veldt on her nightly hunt, her pups warm and safe in the den. Eyes watch her move away; a stealthy shadow detaches itself from the darker shadows and moves towards the den, towards the sleeping pups.

With the spoils of a successful hunt clutched between her jaws the female jackal returns to the scene of a massacre, the den has been opened the bodies of her pups lie scattered all around half eaten, mutilated, blood covering the ground. She drops her bounty her body rigid, ready for flight, but she never stood a chance. The shadow launches itself at the jackal, its strong jaws crushing her skull, tearing her head from her body, now it will eat.

The chilling sound of the howl rips through the night and the only witness to the carnage is the full moon. When the sun claims the day, the vultures will feed and no trace will remain.

Chapter 2

Dust rises in a cloud behind the Land Rover as it makes its way along the narrow dirt road, hiding the other vehicles traveling behind it. At the wheel, Piet's eyes survey the country side, hoping to see some game in the area; he thinks to himself it has been awhile since he has seen a kudu with a decent set of horns, and since he has hung his own biltong.

David and Adele are traveling in a second hand Land Cruiser that David managed to pick up in Lusaka from a used car dealer for a very good price. The man was very happy to accept cash, after all, this vehicle was high-jacked in South Africa and driven across the border and business was booming, although that was a small detail that he omitted to tell David. They had bought a tent, sleeping bags, cots and other basic necessities that they would need. Adele is ready for her big African adventure.

Behind the Land Cruiser, is a 20-ton truck, loaded with everything that they could think of in order to renovate the house and make it livable again. Along with a gang of laborers that Piet had rounded up to do the manual labor with a promise of tobacco, beer, and food, plus a few shillings in the pocket once the job was done.

They crest a hill and look over a vast open veldt. They watch the dark cold slow moving water of the Kafue River glinting in the sunlight. A high kopje overlooking the house from behind throws shadows across the bush and the house itself looking so alone in the vast expanse of the bush veldt. They could see a few dilapidated outbuildings near the house but apart from that, nothing but bush. Adele feels a tremor run up her spine, is it a prickle of fear or excitement she feeling? She glanced at David to check his reaction to what they were seeing. He feels her gaze fall on him and looks back at her, his eyes full of joy. "This is going to be our home darling it needs quite a bit of work but once that's complete you'll find yourself falling in love with it. I know it doesn't look like much right now, but it's all ours to do with as we please."

David had inherited the small farm from his late grandfather, although the old man only stayed there for three months before moving off. He had been unable to sell the farm so as David was his only living relative, the small farm automatically passed on to him.

***

With the sun slowly sinking on the horizon the night sounds fill her ears as Adele sits by the fire and looks around the camp. The tents are up work has started on the house and the air smells fresh and clean. She has had her first bush shower this evening, a ten-gallon bucket with holes in the bottom suspended from the branch of a tree filled with water, heated by the fire. To protect her modesty and give her privacy the sides of an old army tent was put up around the shower area.

With a sigh of contentment, Adele sits back sipping her drink. She watches David and Piet busy at the cooking fire preparing supper. She listens to the chatter of the laborers as they busy themselves around their own cooking fire and watches as the moon no longer full climbs back up into the sky.

Marveling at the night sky, so bright with stars, something she has never seen back in London Adele closes her eyes just drifting along with the smells and sounds of the camp, letting Africa wash over her like the waves of the ocean.

She hears the laughter of the men gathered around the cooking fires and feels at peace with the world. Nothing can hurt her out here, she's safe and content. The meal arrives, pap and vleis as Piet calls it, it smells good and suddenly she realizes just how hungry she is. The conversation turns to the house and the small farm which is more of a smallholding than a farm.

"Hey David, you know, something funny happened in town when I was trying to get this group together, none of the local okes wanted the job. All these guys come from another district, maybe they are just too lazy huh, come to think about it there is something strange about this place of yours."

"Come on Piet, let's not hear your ghost stories tonight, Adele and I are bushed and I can hear our sleeping bags calling us."

"No man, I tell you, something is really strange. You know your oupa planted mielies here before he moved back to town and these now grow wild but there's a troop of baboons that live on the kopje behind you, and not once have I seen them or any other animal in the vicinity of this house. It's just strange man, strange."

"Maybe it's the smell of man that still lingers in the area that keeps them away?"

"*Ag nou praat jy twak,* the human smell would not linger for three years, my friend. It's long gone, no there's something about the place that does not feel right but I can't put my finger on it, bloody hell I have not even seen a bird in the trees today."

"With all the activity going on, maybe that scared the birds off."

"*Nee* Adele, Ag I mean no that would not keep them away, come to think of it, it would be perfect for the weaver to nest here but look around nothing. Oh, and one more thing, there is nothing more stunning than a full moon over the African bush."

The fire dies down, and the camp sleeps soundly to the sound of crickets and frogs. Adele's first night in the African bush passes peacefully.

Chapter 3

Slowly things start to take shape, the generator is repaired and in working order, the chicken houses have been rebuilt ready for their new tenants as this is how David and Adele will supplement the trust fund left to him by his parents. Supplying eggs and chickens to the local supermarket in the nearby town which is 30 km away. The house is coming along nicely and the thatch roof had been replaced, new wiring installed, new plumbing, new kitchen door but not yet ready for David and Adele to move in.

Much to Adele's disappointment she still has to use the outhouse when nature calls but as she tells herself, it's far better than her first night when a hole was dug for her and David stood watch while she completed her toilet.

The bush shower is still in use, as pipes still have to be laid from the mighty Kafue River to feed water to the reservoir which in turn will supply the house, and to the outside irrigation system. David pointed out that they will use nature to supply the water by using gradient pressure.

A gas system will ensure that the house has hot water and electricity will be supplied to the house from the generator. When the generator is not in use, they will use gas or paraffin lanterns for light and the stove and fridge will operate on gas.

David and Piet left early in the morning leaving Adele behind as she did not feel like the 30 km drive into town if you could call it that. A small place called Kafue, 50 km from the hustle and bustle of Lusaka; it has two petrol stations, one motel in town, one just outside of town, and not much else, so she remained behind at the house with the laborers for company, knowing that they would return before mid-day.

Nature calls and Adele cringes at the thought of having to use the outhouse again. She has tried to use it early in the morning and at night when it's cooler and the flies aren't so bad. She crosses the area from the tents, no one sees her. She knocks on the door, not expecting an answer as the two men are in town.

She opens the door and looks into the gloom of the tiny room, steps across the threshold determined to conquer the negative feelings she has regarding the use of this primitive toilet. As Adele seats herself, her eyes adjust to the gloom and she becomes aware that she is not alone. Her visitor is not going to be going anywhere soon.

Draped across the top of the door is the deadliest snake in Africa, a Black Mamba lies there. The only motion from the snake is its small head moving slowly from side to side, its tongue testing the air.

Adele stifles a scream that rises in her throat, she feels the bile rush up and threatens to choke her. She swallows her breathing coming in rapid gasps and she feels as if her heart is now in her mouth. Sweat breaks out all over her body; she feels hot and realizes that she's starting to hyperventilate.

This can't happen, if she hyperventilates she'll lose control and if she loses control she stands a very good chance of being bitten, and with no one to help her she's on her own.

The snake moves slowly along the top of the door in no rush to go anywhere. Adele slows her breathing, her eyes never leaving the unwelcome visitor, and time moves on. She has no idea of time as she does not wear a wrist watch; she's stuck and too scared to move.

Realization sinks in that she needs to stay as still as possible, and not attract the snake's attention which is a bit hard when you are sitting bare butt on the seat of a long drop toilet, as they are not built for comfort.

Blazing heat from the sun beats down mercilessly turning the outhouse into a mini sauna. Sweat runs into her eyes, and burns, her shirt sticks to her body, her nose itches, she has the urge to cough but manages to swallow, her throat dry, feeling like sandpaper.

The temperature radiating off the iron walls is now intense, and Adele starts to feel faint. She's slowly dehydrating and the snake has made no move to leave. Then in the distance, she hears the roar of a motor and the sound of a vehicle entering the yard.

The old thermometer attached to the trunk of an old tree reads 38 degrees in the shade. In a foggy distance, she hears David's voice shouting. "Adele, we're home, Adele where are you?"

She's too scared to return his call, too scared to attract the attention of the unwelcome visitor that's in the outhouse with her.

Piet asks, "Where's the madam? *Kom, kom, kom, Praat julle*, she could be in trouble."

Adele hears the voices in a haze, the heat in the outhouse is slowly shutting her down, then the snake moves, its head coming up its body coiling, footsteps outside the door. "Adele, are you in there?" She tries to talk, but only a croak comes out, "Snake." Both men freeze in their tracks.

"Shut up man, David I think she's in the *kleinhuis, daar's iets fout*; I think I heard the word snake."

The snake is now on full alert, with the sound of voices coming from outside. "Adele, where's the snake, can you tell us?"

With supreme effort, Adele fights against the darkness threatening to overcome her. "The door... on top." With that, the heat in the outhouse takes its toll and Adele slumps on the throne passed out.

Voices in the distance, the cool feel of fresh air on her body, Adele slowly comes around, to find herself on her cot in the shade of a tree with David and Piet by her side. David is wiping her brow with a wet cloth trying to bring her body temperature down. Piet offers her a drink but pulls it back as she starts to gulp the cool liquid.

"*Nee* sister, slowly, drink it slowly, your body will reject it if you drink too fast."

She remembers the snake and shudders at the memory. "The snake, what happened to the snake?"

"Piet took care of it, once we realized that you had passed out and the bloody thing would not see you as a threat, he and two of the boys, Adam and Calvin armed themselves with sticks. Opened the door, and the snake came out like an express train but the guys were ready, the score, snake, nil and guys, one."

"Ja Adele, you were very lucky and also you had the presence of mind to stay where you were. That *blikskim* was a bloody Black Mamba and not small either. This bugger measured just less than 3 meters, one bite and it would have been *totsiens* to you young lady."

"Piet, I think that we need to take Adele in hand and give her shooting lessons, teach her to use the 303 rifle as well as the 9 mil browning. Adele, you can carry the 9 mil with you at all times, remember we are in the bush, anything can happen."

Chapter 4

Morning arrives with the brilliant glare of the sun and the camp starts moving like a well-oiled machine. Work on the house is going at a relatively fast pace and it looks as if they will soon be able to move into their renovated home.

The three of them converge on the rubbish dump at the back of the house where Piet has set up beer bottles at different distances, ranging from 10 m to 100 m.

"Okay sweetheart, let me show you how the bolt action on this 303 works and remember, set the butt of the rifle tight inside your armpit so the recoil will not bruise you."

"David honey you men are all the same assuming that the damsel is in distress, pass the rifle here. Let me show you something."

Adele takes the rifle from David. Piet moves behind her for safety sake, ready to hug the ground as he does not trust a firearm in the hands of a woman.

The woman handles the weapon like a pro. Sights at the bottle 100 m away, squeeze the trigger, the rifle barks and the bottle shatters. She fires again, and another bottle shatters. The sound of the rifle bounces back at them from the kopje behind them, breaking the still morning air. No birds take flight from the nearby trees, there are no birds.

Both men watch her mouths agape in surprise. Who would think that a delicate English flower could shoot like that? She exchanges the rifle for the 9 mil Browning and finishes off the remaining bottles in a flurry. The whole exercise takes less than 5 minutes to destroy all 12 bottles that Piet had set up.

With a sly smile and a twinkle in her eyes, Adele turns towards the two gaping men. "Thank you gentleman, that was fun now where's breakfast?" Both men are stunned by her performance. "Bloody hell Adele, how and where did you learn to shoot like that?" "Adele, honey, you're a woman of many talents, and I never knew you could shoot."

"Well you never asked me, you just assumed that because I'm a woman I didn't know how, but let me tell you a secret. My Dad was a marine and as a young girl, I use to go to the shooting range with him. He taught me how to shoot and take care of firearms so you have no need to worry about me guys. I'm able to take care of myself unless of course I'm trapped in a toilet."

"Right darling, that's true and we apologize for that. Come on breakfasts on me, who wants coffee?" With a shake of his head in wonder, Piet decides the occasion needs something stronger. "Ag man, not me, after that display, I need a beer."

The broken glass glitters in the sunlight, the aftermath of Adele's shooting performance.

***

The three make their way back to the tent area, where the conversation turns to how David and Piet met and became best friends. The two of them grew up in South Africa in a small town called Amanzimtoti on the South Coast of KwaZulu-Natal. Piet, being Afrikaans went to *Kuswag Hoërskool,* and David went to Kingsway High. They both played cricket for their schools, and although on opposing teams became firm friends, from cycling to school together to double dating.

Employment in South Africa was at an all-time low under the government of the ANC. Piet being an adventurer moved around until he settled in Zambia.

David had the luxury of his trust fund so an income wasn't important to him and he had the travel bug, which is how he ended up in the UK and met Adele.

Both men stayed in contact over the years, and when David inherited the small holding it gave him a reason to move back to Africa, and once again team up with Piet.

***

The party is loud, the braai fire is lit and the beer flows like the Kafue River. The celebration of the completion of the house is in full swing. Piet will return to his Safari Business in the morning and the laborers will return home with money in their pockets, a hangover and plenty of Boxer tobacco.

Adam has volunteered to stay on at the smallholding living in one of the buildings that have been converted for that purpose. He will assist with the upkeep of the chickens, as well as maintain the grounds around the house as there is a lot of bush that has encroached over the last three years onto the area around the house, and needs to be cleared.

Adele has developed a fear of snakes thanks to her near miss in the Long Drop, and who can blame her. She wants the area cleared.

Chickens had arrived the day before and had taken up residence in their new home. The chicken houses had been rebuilt, new mesh had been installed, feeding troughs totally redone and David and Adele were set for business in the egg and chicken trade.

The house itself is now ready for the newlyweds with running water, a toilet that flushes electricity from the generator, which has been designed to start and switch off from the house. So there is no need for David or Adam to have to crack the handle to get it fired up, and this has been achieved but using a car battery, attached to the generator.

Furniture arrived the day before along with a big double bed, gas stove and fridge, and it now seems as if the house is saying, "Live in me."

Morning comes and it's full of goodbyes. The laborers leave in the truck still drunk from the night before. The sound of singing follows them as they leave, heading back to Kafue and their families.

Piet stands by his Land Rover ready for the long trip back to Lusaka. "You guys take it easy out here hey. Remember this is not London or Lusaka, this is the bush my friends and if you need me, you've got my cell number. Just remember to charge your bloody phones when you run the genny and watch out for each other. Man I love both of you, Adele I just met you, but I love you too."

"Cheers Piet, thanks for all the assistance. Drive carefully my friend and don't be a stranger. Give me a call when you get to Lusaka."

Dust billows out from behind the Land Rover as Piet follows the road home. They stand in the yard until they can't hear the sound of the motor anymore and the sound of silence descends down on them. Apart from Adam, they realize that they are finally alone, for the first time in three weeks, eventually alone.

Chapter 5

The sound of a vehicle breaks the silence around the house which brings them both out onto the front stoop. Wondering who the visitor is, as everyone has just left but as the vehicle comes into view they realize that it's Piet, making his way back.

He roars into the yard, sending dust devils up into the air, and brings the Land Rover to a sudden halt, jumps out and smiles at their questioning looks.

"Hey *jammer* man, but I have been thinking and this is bugging me. There is something not right here and I can't put my finger on it. Not once in the time we have been here have I seen anything to shoot, no game near this bloody house, no birds in the trees."

"Piet hey slow down, you're scaring Adele, take it, easy man. Let's grab a coffee and you can have your say."

"David, Adele, listen to me, I'm not trying to scare anyone. I'm worried man, it's not natural that there's no bird life around here, look around, it's like paradise here. There should also be small game running around but nothing, fok I don't know man, it's just not right."

"Piet you worry too much, you're acting like a mother hen, and we are your chicks. Look my friend; we have the rifle and the 9 mil. Adam's here with us, the house is secure and we feel safe. Maybe the birds will come. Will you feel better then?"

"Man I'm sorry but you guys are like family to me, I just worry when I can't get an answer. I just felt the need to come back and tell you. What we still need to do is put up a security fence around this property, maybe once that's in place, I'll sleep easier. Tell you what, I'll go into Kafue and buy the fencing, the poles; come back here with one or two other okes. There is still enough cement and put the fencing up then leave you two lovebirds alone, heck not much of a honeymoon, hey Adele?"

"Okay Piet, if that's going to make you feel better, go ahead. We do have a guest room in the house, so that's not a problem, let's do it."

The fence goes up, 8ft high, strong mesh is used and as Piet says, "Only a charging elephant will get through that. Now I feel okay to leave you two alone out here. Ja, nou kan ń man huis toe gaan."

Once again they stand on the stoop and watch the departure of their friend. Adam opens the gate to allow Piet out and they watch the dust settle back onto the road. The silence washes over them; alone they turn and enter their home eager to start their future together.

***

Days pass quickly. Both David and Adele are caught up in the day-to-day running of their smallholding, feeding chickens, collecting eggs and exploring their new home.

Adam is kept busy cutting away brush and clearing the area around the house. His work disturbs a couple of Puff adders which he quickly dispatches with a panga and the mate of the Mamba that held Adele prisoner, which causes a bit of alarm. David is able to kill it with the 9 mil and this one measured just over 3 meters. Slowly things start to take shape around the house and before they know it the weekend is upon them.

"David, I have an idea. We've been cooped up here since we arrived, working and I for one want to see something of the area around our home. So how about we grab those fishing rods Piet left behind and I'll put a picnic lunch together, throw in a couple of beers, and we spend the afternoon down at the river."

"Now you're talking. That sounds like a great idea but we have to remember we are very close to the Kafue National Park, and there could be wild life around. Plus the river has Nile crocodile and pods of hippo so the rifle must come with us, but man, the thought of fresh Tiger fish done on coals is making my mouth water already."

"You know sweetheart, Kafue National Park is Zambia's oldest park and by far the largest. It's the size of Wales and is spread over 22 400 square kilometers, making it one of the largest National Parks in Africa. It's fed by three rivers, the Lufupa in the northwest and the Lunga and Kafue in the north-east which puts us right on its boundary so the possibility of encountering big game is very real. We just have to be very aware of our surroundings."

Slowly and carefully they make their way through the riverside forest down to the banks of the slow moving Kafue River. The security fence is behind them as they leave the sanctuary of their home. David in the lead carrying the food and drink plus a blanket, with Adele following, the rifle slung over her shoulder.

They reach a spot almost directly in line with their house and Adele marvels at how wide the river is. Outcrops of rocks jut out into the slow moving water which looks like a mirror, with the sun reflecting off it. Water reeds growing alongside the river bank, it looks so tranquil, just what Adele had in mind, just the two of them and the river. The spot they select is under the shade of a large tree and they set up their picnic.

"Those rocks seem like a great place to fish from darling, I think I'll go out there and throw a few lines and see what comes up. Oh, baby, you know that in the extreme north of the Kafue lies the Busanga Plains, one of Zambia's most significant wetland resources and one of the few areas in the world that remain untouched by development and human activity. It covers 750 square kilometers of breathtaking wilderness, we must plan a trip there with Piet as it's the best area in Zambia to see cheetah."

"David, you're acting now, just trying to show me how much you know of the area. Show-off, but I love you, so don't stop, I want to learn as much as I can about our new home."

Adele watches as David moves onto the rocks and throws his line, there is not a ripple on the face of the river. She hears the songs of birds in the trees and finds herself thinking back on what Piet had to say and wonders why there is no bird life in the area around the house. What reason could there be?

She hears a rustle in the nearby brush and turns her head in the direction of the noise. Holding her breath she watches as a Defassa waterbuck moves into the clearing about 30 m from them, and starts to drink.

"Hey Adele, is the beer cold yet?" The waterbuck starts at the sudden shout from David and bolts back into the brush. Adele laughs, "David, you're a real jerk, you scared the hell out of that animal."

"What animal? I never saw a thing, sorry baby, I'll check next time before I shout out aloud. Right, I'm ready for a beer or two and then, watch out Tiger fish because here I come."

The heat of the day plus four beers later makes David feels sleepy but he had come down to the river to fish, so fish he does. First casting his line from the closest rock but when there's no bite, moves slowly further out into the river using the jutting rocks as stepping stones, and a point to fish from.

Adele dozes in the shade of the tree, every now and then looking up through half closed lids in order to keep track of her husband.

The singing of the birds in the trees keeps her company as she closes her eyes, her mind far away. Suddenly she's jerked back to reality, her eyes wide open, something's wrong, what? It's too quiet; the birds have fallen silent as if they are waiting for something to happen.

She glances towards David who is about 15 m from the river bank. Standing on a small group of rocks that he has managed to jump to, he's okay. She looks around at the bush around them, nothing but silence, no movement. But the air is now charged with electricity, something is going down, something is not what it seems. Look, look, she tells herself, don't call David; he'll only think that I'm acting like a girl.

Her eyes move back to David and a small ripple in front of where he's standing catches her eye. She studies the ripple and slowly with dawning horror she realizes that David has been added to the dinner menu. He's busy being stalked by a crocodile and is totally unaware of the reptile as his full attention is on fishing.

Chapter 6

Slowly, ever so slowly the Nile crocodile moves towards its intended prey, tail moving just below the surface of the water, silence fills the area as it moves into position to attack.

The sound of the rifle shot echo's across the river, the crocodile arches out of the water in a macabre dance of death, blood spraying from the bullet hole between its eyes. David turns at the sound of the shot, to see his wife standing at the edge of the river bank, rifle in hand, aiming in his direction. Another shot, he spins around expecting to feel the tug of a bullet slamming into him, only to see the dead croc pop to the surface of the river, blood running from two bullet wounds, one between the eyes, and the second just behind the head. He finds himself slipping on the rocks, over balances and falls into the water. The fishing rods forgotten slowly bob up and down on the surface as they join the current and are swept away.

Adam comes flying onto the scene, armed with his precious panga, David pulls himself out of the river onto the bank and Adele runs to him, relief written all over her face. "I thought that I was done for, that you were trying to kill me, thank God I married a woman who can shoot."

It takes the two men a good hour to drag the body of the croc out of the water and onto the river bank. It measures just over 5 m long from the tip of its snout to its tail, and the approximate weight of it is about 270 kg, and to confirm everything, Adele's first shot killed the reptile.

Together they manage to drag the body high enough from the water's edge and secure it to a tree with the hopes that the smell of death will not attract any scavengers or any of its relatives on the lookout for an easy meal. David wants to contact Piet and get him to come and take the body away, as Piet can use the croc to put some money in his bank account.

Adam returns from the house with a roll of chicken wire, which they place over the dead croc, in order to protect the skin from any unwanted visitors, and secures it with tent pegs driven into the ground.

They make their way back to the house, and David makes that call to Piet using the cell phone, and although the signal is not very good, the story is related to Piet, who promises to be at the smallholding by first light.

***

After the sun sets on the horizon, a new full moon claims the night sky, illuminating the world below it with a lunar light, throwing out shadows from the trees and bushes.

David and Adele sleep, the sleep of the dead, both totally wasted from the close brush with death, wrung out emotionally, but not a care in the world. Safe and sound in the knowledge that they are secure in their home they fail to hear the terrified commotion coming from the chicken houses.

Adam hears, but will not venture out into the darkness, he cowers under his covers and prays to his gods, finally, all is silent, and he too succumbs to what his body desperately needs sleep.

***

Piet is true to his word, the sun has no sooner peeked onto the land of the living when he arrives at the smallholding in a cloud of dust, a crew of his employees with him to deal with the dead croc, all hyped up and ready to go. After all, all Piet wants is the skin, and the head, which means that there's plenty of croc meat to go around, so tonight we eat until our bellies swell.

David meets him at the back door, still red eyed from a deep sleep. "Jeez Piet, when you say first light, you mean first light, we haven't even had coffee yet. Come in, Adele's busy getting dressed she'll join us soon, man it's a lucky thing that she can shoot, that bastard was almost on top of me."

Adam moves across the yard to the kitchen where the two men are talking, he looks very uneasy, and not very sure of himself, holding his peak cap in his hands, he shuffles forward until David notices him. "Morning Adam, what's wrong?"

"There was something wrong last night, the chickens, they made a lot of noise, but I was too scared to check because of the darkness, and the blood moon. I have checked on them this morning, and all is alright, but there's another problem, the fence has been damaged near the rubbish dump."

"Blood moon, what's that Adam?"

Piet takes charge, his face grim as he recalls the myths and superstitions of the Blood Moon

.

"Ag okay, let me handle this Adam, David a blood moon is when the moon is full, and the local superstition amongst the tribes here believe that when it's a full moon, the creatures of the night walk upright and reign terror on anyone who's stupid enough to be out in the open. They believe that this is when the dead walk, and prey on the living. It's a big thing in witchcraft, and the witch doctors use this for their own gain, but it's a bloody load of nonsense, but these people, they believe it."

They move across the yard, to the rubbish dump, to inspect the damage. From what they can see, the damage has been inflicted from the inside of the property.

Piet stands back and surveys the damage in awe.

"Man, *wat gaan hier aan?* This is a bloody strong fence; I told you a *bliksem* bull elephant would have to charge to break this. Never mind let my guys repair this while we have coffee and wait for the lady of the house, the croc isn't going anywhere, and we need to investigate this fence, and try to puzzle this out."

Piet and David, along with Adam check the area around the broken section of fencing, but can't find anything to point towards the culprit, no one notices the mangled corpse of the Rock Rabbit or the drops of blood near the rubbish dump, leading to the damaged fence, all three men are baffled at what could have gone through, and the wind whips up the dust, hiding the blood droplets from sight.

Chapter 7

They make their way through the forest, towards the river bank where the body of the croc waits. They walk behind the singing gang of laborers, who's only thought, is of all the croc meat they are going to take home. The sound of the singing carries, it's a good feeling all around as they move down the slope towards the river.

The safari crew is the first ones to exit the brush and lay eyes on the dead croc. The singing is choked back, to be replaced by loud gasps of disbelief at what they see. David, Piet, and Adele join the crew; Adele covers her mouth and stumbles over to a bush where she vomits out her breakfast.

David and Piet look at the scene before them in shocked horror at what they see, the crew starts talking about witchcraft, glancing around at the bush, scared. Adele re-joins them white faced and horrified at the carnage.

"*En now, wat sê kak* do we have here? Bloody hell David, I don't know what could have done this to Adele's croc."

The wire mesh has been ripped from the body of the croc, and the whole area looks as if a bloody battle has been fought there. The body of the croc has been torn apart, its intestines are thrown into the tree, the rope holding it to the tree, broken in half, and its head was torn from its body, parts of its body reduced to pulp. It's as if something or someone took great pleasure in just totally destroying the remains of the croc.

Piet moves forward to get a better look. *"Bly waar julle is,* I want to check for spoor."* He approaches what is left of the croc, eyes to the ground "Bloody hell, did one of you walk here before we got here?" His crew, now wide eyed, and looking terrified assures him, that not one of them had been near the croc.

"Okay you guys, secure the area, there's nothing here that we can use, but we need to get Oom Hennie out here to have a look at this. David, I need to talk to you and Adele, back at the house where these guys can't hear us."

Following Piet back to the house, the group settles on the front stoop.

"Guys, I don't have an answer for what we saw down at the river, but one thing I can tell you is that whatever did that to the croc leaves a spoor, almost like a humans, that's is why Oom Hennie must be called, he has worked in forensics all his life, and maybe he can identify what tore up that croc of yours."

"What about the fence, quite a bit of damage was done?"

"Must have been someone or something that got trapped here behind the fence, and fear gave it the strength to break through, remember there's been no fence here, and suddenly a barrier."

"What about the croc, you think maybe some villagers took revenge on it? I heard that a woman was taken a few days ago upriver by a croc."

"It's possible, but remember, last night was the first full moon, and not many of them will be found out in the dark, but ja, it's the only reasonable explanation that makes sense, and that will explain the spoor that I saw, but let's wait for Oom Hennie to arrive, and not jump to any conclusions just yet."

Piet makes the call to Lusaka and puts his request to Hennie, who works with the local police department as a pathologist and also doubles up in forensic science. Once Piet has described the scene to him, he assures Piet that he'll be at the smallholding by midday.

"I'm not happy guys this place feels strange, and suddenly doesn't feel right, I don't know, maybe this bloody full moon is playing tricks with my mind, but just to make me happy, put a padlock on your gate at night."

Adam approaches the group on the stoop, looking very unhappy. "Ja Adam, what's the problem?"

"I have been talking to the others, and they say that we need to leave this place, this place is cursed, and that if we stay bad things will happen."

"*Nee, nee, nee,* man, that bunch of mine is talking rubbish; they are playing with your mind to scare you. Mr. David and Ms.

Adele need you here. The chickens could have been upset by anything, a lynx, or maybe a leopard, no Adam, stay here with them man."

"Mr. Piet, Mr. David, I will stay, but please can you give me a hunting torch so that I can see in the dark, and another lock on my door?"

Chapter 8

As they wait for the arrival of the pathologist, they walk around the perimeter of the security fencing, David and Piet testing points here and there, they check on the repaired section, and both men are satisfied. Their wandering's around the smallholding ends up at the chicken houses, which according to Piet look very secure that not even a Leopard would be able to get in

The sound of the vehicle carries to them across the vast open bush, and they can see the dust cloud being thrown up behind it as it makes its way towards them, and into the yard.

Oom Hennie is a small man, bald and wearing thick lens glasses, and Adele puts his age beyond retirement. It comes out in small talk that Oom Hennie does this for the love of the job, and not the money, but the truth is he's alone and the job is what keeps him going

The group once again move through the gate and down towards the river to the area where the remains of the croc are.

Oom Hennie is unable to hide his expression of shock at what he sees before him, but being the professional that he is, he puts that behind him and gets to work. Photos are taken of the area, of the spoor around the croc, of the damage done to the body, he takes samples from various parts of the croc and bags them, explaining that he will be doing tests for saliva on them to try to determine what's responsible.

The spoor intrigues him as it looks like a human footprint.

He completes his examination of the body and area, and informs David and Piet that he has everything he needs; he assures them that he should have the results back from the tests in about two weeks, and will let them know who the visitor was as soon as he has been able to do the identification.

Oom Hennie suggests that the remains get thrown into the river so as not to attract any predators or scavengers that might be in the area. Piet barks out the order, and the gang begins the grisly task of cleaning up

A tuft of hair is played with by the gentle breeze that comes off the river. The hair has been caught in the tree, on a branch about 6 ft above the ground, as it would if someone or something brushed up against it, and is caught in the bark.

No one sees it, it's only a tuft, and it's not human. It was not there the day the croc was shot.

***

The day moves on, Oom Hennie and Piet have left, the smallholding shimmers under the African sun with dust devils playing in the veldt, the air is heavy and in the distance storm, clouds gather.

The wind picks up, racing around the buildings, whispering to anyone who takes the time to listen. The roll of thunder bounces off the kopje behind the house, lightning flashes like God taking a photo in the sky and the clouds blot out the sun, claiming the heavens for their own.

Day darkens as the storm gathers momentum, the wind builds to a deafening howl as it rushes between the trees and buildings, and David and Adele watch as the curtain of rain rushes towards them. This is their first African storm, and they watch in amazement as the lightning forks down to earth, and the thunder hammers out its own drum beat.

The rain drops are heavy, and thunder into the dry dusty earth around their home, turning it into mud in a matter of minutes.

Adam shivers in his room, he knows that the storm will howl all night long, and tonight, there will be no full moon as the sky has been claimed by the storm god, and he can sleep easy, as nothing will move while the storm rages, and the moon is not visible.

Morning brings with it, the clean smell of the fresh air, dust free, washed clean by the storm. All traces of blood droplets at the rubbish dump and surrounding area have now been wiped away; the tuft of hair down at the river bank is gone.

It's as if nature has decided to clean up, there's no evidence of the violence that took place; all is still and quiet and the bright African sun looks down, slowly drying the remains of the storm.

Chapter 9

A noise comes to him in his sub-conscious. David, in a deep sleep once again hears the sound, and he struggles to rise to the surface of sleep. Fighting to come awake, hearing but not knowing where it's coming from or what it is.

Adele stirs beside him, and suddenly both are wide awake, the sound of terrified chickens breaking through the darkness of their bedroom, splitting the still of the night with sounds of terror.

He falls out of bed, hands shaking as he tries to light the gas lamp. The only light is from the full moon now heading towards the other side of the earth and falling from its position in the night sky. It is just after 3 am in the morning, and it sounds as if the gates of hell have been opened.

The light from the gas lamp pushes back the darkness in the room. David lunges for the 303 rifle, and stumbles from the room towards the kitchen, thumbing the safety off as he moves forward. Rushing towards the unknown and the darkness outside with Adele behind him, flashlight at the ready, wide eyed and scared.

The sounds die down as they reach the kitchen; silence descends down on the smallholding. It's only the sound of their heavy breathing that can be heard. Slowly he works the bolt of the safety lock on the stable door, its sliding sounds as loud as the thunder the day before. He disengages the Yale lock, and with a shaking hand opens the top of the door, to look out at darkness towards the chicken houses.

The light from the moon is no longer bright, and Adele stabs the darkness with the bright beam of the flashlight. She moves the beam slowly towards the shadows, cutting through the darkness. Both of them peering out into the early morning gloom, where shadows rule.

David's hands are clammy with sweat on the rifle as he tries to see beyond the veil of the dark that covers the area around the chicken houses. Nothing moves and the shadows retreat from the beam of light as Adele searches the ground. All is quiet as they stand in the doorway looking out. She plays the beam across the chicken houses, and they see the damage, the fronts have been torn off, and the bodies of chickens lie scattered all over the yard. David opens the bottom half of the door and eases out into the yard.

"Stay here baby, just keep the torch light ahead of me, I'm going to check on Adam, and try seeing what's happened."

Holding the rifle, ready to fire at anything that moves, he cautiously moves barefoot across the yard in the direction of the chicken houses and Adam's room. Chickens lie in his path, torn apart, blood splatters the walls of the building, feathers are all over the place, total carnage has taken place and there is not a living thing to be seen. Adele joins him, so much for staying inside, but he welcomes her company, and they both inspect the area in the light thrown from the torch.

They move towards Adam's room, barefoot, feeling the earth under them and approach his door. "Adam, are you there, are you alright?"

No answer, David tries the door and it opens easily, he peers into the room, it's empty. Adam's belongings are there, but Adam's missing.

They shout for him, but the only answer they get is the echo off the kopje behind them, Adam has left or he can't hear them. They move back to the house, realizing that there's not much they can do until daylight, but they must call Piet and the police for assistance. David is out of his depth here, and he knows it.

They close the stable door and lock it. From the shadows near the rubbish dump, a pair of eyes watches as the door closes.

***

Morning has broken, and with it, David and Adele survey the damage that was caused in the early hours of the morning, neither of them had been able to go back to sleep, they were too hyped-up by what had taken place, and both on edge. The chickens had been decimated, the fittings meant to protect them from predators torn from their holdings, but most of all, the disappearance of Adam is foremost on their minds. They had ventured out again to check his room, but nothing was out of place his bed had been slept in, but his torch and panga were missing. They could find nothing missing from his room.

There was nothing they could do until Piet, along with the police arrived, and hopefully would be able to provide some answers.

Both parties arrive on top of each other, much to the relief of David and Adele, as the total silence surrounding the smallholding was starting to fray their nerves. Sgt Dube, from the police task force in Lusaka, arrived with four constables; Piet arrived with his nephew, Andrew a young man of 23, eager to follow in his uncle's footsteps, and his tracker, all armed and ready for action thinking that a leopard could be the culprit, and was very eager for a hunt.

Sgt Dube sent his constables to scout around, outside the perimeter fence to see if they could track down Adam, as it was possible he had taken fright last night and decided that discretion is better than valor and taken to higher ground. He along with Piet and the tracker survey the area around the chicken houses, with David and Adele staying in the background so as not to get in the way

"*Nee daar's fokall hier*, David, the only spoor that we can see is a bloody footprint where you and Adele were, if there was anything, it's been walked over."

The damage and the carnage to the chicken houses, and chickens baffles them, the way the wire had been ripped off, and the chickens tore apart could only have been done by something with very strong jaws, something that kills for pure pleasure.

"Maybe a male from that troop of mountain baboons paid a visit, but I can't' be sure as all traces of spoor have been walked over and..." A shout of alarm comes from the far side of the property.

"Sgt Dube, we've found something over here."

Lying on the ground, outside the fencing is the flashlight that was given to Adam, it lens smashed, and close by it the panga. On closer inspection, it's very clear that the blade of the panga has traces of blood on it.

The area around both articles had not been disturbed, which means they were thrown over the fence, in order for them to end up where they were found. Sgt Dube slips on a pair of latex gloves and slips both objects into evidence bags.

The men double their efforts in the search, now positive that something has happened to Adam, and slowly move down towards the river, spreading out and scanning the brush and trees as they move, covering as wide an area as they can. David and Adele make up the numbers of the searchers, but their efforts go unrewarded, and they return to the smallholding defeated.

The search now moves to inside the security fence, starting from the right of the building, moving to the left towards the chicken houses, and Adam's room. Beyond that, the generator room and the rubbish dump.

The men are very methodical in their search, looking for any clue that could point a way to Adam, they move past his room, towards the rubbish dump, and there they see it, and what they see makes hardened policemen stop in their tracks, the bile rising in their throats, Sgt Dube makes a frantic call for backup.

Adam's body lies on top of the dump; he has been decapitated, and disemboweled, the flies already buzzing around his stiffening corpse. Adele stumbles back; the color draining from her face, David and Piet look on in horror, Sgt Dube loses his breakfast.

Adam's head has been placed in the opening of his chest, his dead eyes wide open, and his face frozen in an expression of utter terror, with his tongue lying discarded alongside his remains. With a shake of his head Piet turns to David, "*Ja Boet*, now we know why you did not hear any screams...some fucking thing ripped his tongue out."

Chapter 10

Oom Hennie arrives at the smallholding, which has now been turned into a crime scene, and together with his forensic team, they start to comb the area around the dump looking for any clues that will lead them to the answers that they need.

Adam's body is photographed, bagged and then removed to the pathologist's van for removal to the state morgue in Lusaka, where further tests, plus an autopsy will be performed in order to determine the time of death, as well as how he died.

Overzealous police are all over David and Adele, question after question, trying to trip them up with a lie, trying to tie them in with Adams death, but both of them stick to the truth and repeat it over and over to the investigating officer. They are interviewed separately, and both stories are identical, which leaves the police with nowhere to go, and no suspect in Adam's death.

The coroner, aka Oom Hennie, has not yet ruled Adams death as murder or misadventure as no tests have yet been conducted on the body, but the police in Zambia are very quick to jump to conclusions in their haste to close a case.

By mid-afternoon, the investigation around the smallholding and immediate surrounding area outside the security fence has been concluded, and nothing of any other significance had been uncovered.

The police leave in convoy with Oom Hennie at the rear. Before leaving, he assures all three of them that the tests on the croc will be available soon, and he will get in touch, and will also advise them on what comes out of the investigation and what the results are from tests run on Adam's body.

Piet is not happy, and both David and Adele are feeling very uneasy about staying on the smallholding after all that has happened. Piet gets his guys to burn the remains of the chickens, while the two newlyweds pack a suitcase, and secure the house.

All three feel that a week or two off the smallholding and away from the violence that has reared its head in their lives will do them a world of good, and during that time, Oom Hennie might have some answers for them.

Piet is certain that a mountain baboon was responsible for the chicken slaughter, but when it comes to Adam's death, he's as stumped as everyone else involved, but as they all know; time will tell.

With the setting sun in the west, the two vehicles head towards the town of Kafue, while the full moon makes it way slowly up towards the point from where it rules the earth at night, and the house stands alone, silent and empty in the growing dark.

***

Two weeks pass quickly for David and Adele, and the events at the smallholding slowly recede into the back of their minds, and they find themselves looking forward to returning to their home and starting over again. David has had the chicken houses repaired while they have been away, and has made arrangements for a new consignment of birds to be delivered, the day after they anticipate taking up residence again.

Piet has introduced them to the lady in his life. Peggy is a slender brunette of 32, who works as a teller at Barclays Banks in Lusaka, and both women hit it off right away, which was great as it now means that Piet is not the odd one out, and Adele has a woman friend in the area.

Adele had insisted that they get a dog, not only to act as an early warning system on the smallholding but to be company as well, so off to the local SPCA. That's where they meet Bodger, a fully grown Bull Mastiff, who captures her heart with his mournful eyes, ready wag of the stump of his tail and eager to join the family.

The only down side to the trip to Lusaka was the feedback received from Oom Hennie regarding the croc, as well as the report on the death of Adam. He contacted them and advised them that there's a possibility that the slides got mixed up with some other work that he's busy with, and he has to start all over again, as the only thing that has come up from the saliva tests is that of a Spotted Hyena had been at both bodies. It was possible that the Hyena had been at the corpse of the croc, feeding, but not responsible for the damaged caused, it was impossible that a hyena had come into contact with Adam, and was responsible for his death due to the body being found inside the secured area. He promises them that he would expedite his investigation into both cases, and let them have his findings as soon as possible.

Adams death had been ruled as misadventure, although the cause was still undetermined, which meant that David and Adele were no longer considered as persons of interest by the police. The police had returned to the smallholding, in order to conduct further investigations, and had been attacked by a fully grown male baboon, which they shot.

It turned out to be a Chacma Baboon, that had been kicked out of the troop that inhabited the kopje and gone rogue, its weight was 45 kg and the length of its canine teeth was 3.86 cm which made him the perfect candidate for the attack on the chickens.

As far as Adam's death is concerned, the police are also waiting for the findings from the coroner's office, as they had reached a dead end out at the smallholding.

Chapter 11

They return to the smallholding, to find all well and intact as they had left it. Bodger takes to his new home like a duck to water and spends most of the first day investigating all the new smells, but one incident stands out in Adele's mind, the dog's reaction to the rubbish dump. His hair stands on end, and a low growl issues forth from the back of his throat, stiff legged and ready to fight, but with what? She can't see anything that could have caused such a response from him. She calls him, but the dog ignores her, his eyes riveted on the rubbish dump, and then slowly he backs up until he turns and runs to her, his body quivering and muscles tense, the hair slowly relaxing. David thinks it could be a snake, but on investigation, there's nothing that could have caused such a response from the dog.

The chickens arrive and are installed in their new home. This time around strong mesh wire has been used in their home, along with steel bars set horizontally into the brick work to make it near impossible for anything to get at them, and as an added plus, they now have Bodger to watch over them.

Night falls, and once again the arrival of the full moon. One month has passed since the death of Adam, and the attack on the chickens. There has still been no feedback from Oom Hennie, and both David and Adele are starting to relax, feeling as if the worst is now past them, and they can now concentrate on establishing themselves, and more importantly, start the family that Adele so desperately wants, so with the full face of the moon shining down on the smallholding, they make their way down the passage to the bedroom.

Sounds of vicious barking split the stillness of the night and wake David with a start, for a few seconds he's not quite sure where he is, Adele shakes him. "David, it's Bodger, something's wrong."

They hear low growls coming from the back yard, followed by more barks. David grabs the rifle and runs down the passage to the kitchen with Adele on his heels holding the flash light in one hand, and the 9 mil in the other.

On reaching the kitchen the growling stops, followed by a series of barks, and then silence. David cautiously opens the door and looks out across the yard, when suddenly a shadow moves to his right towards him. The rifle comes up, the finger already squeezing the trigger, the shot rings out as Adele pushes the rifle up, and into his vision trots Bodger, the stump of his tail wagging in greeting.

David slumps against the door frame in relief, the rifle still at the ready. Whatever was out there has been seen off by Bodger. Adele opens the bottom half of the door and invites the dog in, while David plays the strong beam of the torch across the yard, just to convince himself that all is well.

The beam moves towards the area where the rubbish dump is, and beyond the security fence into the brush surrounding the property when the beam reflects off a pair of eyes, looking directly at him, one second they are there, the next they are gone, leaving him to doubt himself, did he really see them? What was it that belonged to the eyes; they were at least 5 ft. from the ground?

This he decides to keep to himself until he has had a chance to look around in the daylight, and possibly have a word with Piet. He closes the door, more shaken than he would admit, and grateful for the company of the Bull Mastiff in the house

The nocturnal visitor watches from the brush as the door closes, and silently moves off on two legs towards the kopje, where it knows the hunting is good, and the young of the baboon is easy prey; the dog, on the other hand, is another matter.

***

David calls Piet, who once again complains about the cell reception, but tells David that he'll be out at their place over the weekend, and would it be okay if he brings Peggy with him and they make a weekend of it. That's no problem, David knows that Adele will be thrilled to have another woman in the house for a change and that there's plenty of room at the Inn.

During the conversation, David recalls the events of the night before to Piet, including the eyes that the beam of light picked up in the brush, as well as the dog's reaction to the rubbish dump. Piet suggests that Bodger sleeps in the house until they manage to establish what's wandering around the property but to keep the firearms close.

"Never you mind my friend; we'll get to the bottom of this. I will bring Oom Hennie's findings with me on Friday, as he has contacted me and told me the results will be ready on Thursday night, so we can all see what is what, and decide on our next plan of action. I think that there's mischief about, and maybe the locals want the two of you gone. But hey, ń Boer maak ń plan, so don't worry, ou Piet has got a thing or two up his sleeve."

That night, both of them are woken to the sound of furious growling and barking coming from the vicinity of the kitchen. David with a rifle in hand stumbles into the kitchen to find a very upset dog standing at the back door, the growls low in his throat, his hair standing on end and a very angry Bull Mastiff ready to take on all comers. Adele joins him, armed with the pistol, ready to shoot anything that moves. She's calm as she tells David to let the dog out.

He unlocks the door and no sooner is it opened than Bodger bolts from the house, into the darkness outside, ferocious growls emitting from his throat as he charges across the yard towards the chicken houses. Adele follows his charge with the torch, while David keeps the rifle trained on the dog. The light of the full moon is not enough to illuminate the yard, but strong enough to throw shadows in every direction.

David senses movement to the right of the dog, and fires the rifle, he hears the thud of the bullet striking something, and hears the rapid movement of something scaling the security fence, Adele throws the beam of light towards the sound, but they can see nothing.

The night is silent as they stare out into the darkness that surrounds them, only to be broken by the stab of light from the torch as Adele moves it from right to left and back again, searching for the source of the dog's anger, and for the thing that scaled the fence.

Dead silence is suddenly broken by the haunting sound of a howl; Adele plays the light towards the source, only to discover their dog, on his haunches howling at the moon.

An answering howl that comes from the darkness makes their hair stand on end.

Chapter 12

Next morning, David and Adele have a look around in the general direction that he fired the rifle, and soon discover the source of the thud that they had heard. David's bullet had hit one of the support poles of the fence. They check the ground around the fence and the only sign that anything had been there were the odd one or two human foot prints. Bodger's hackles rise once again, and low growls come from the dog at the sight of the spoor in the sand.

Both agree to wait until Piet arrives before they take any more action. It's obvious that David's shot missed whatever was there, but that the sound of the rifle scared it off, which in a small way is a comfort to them

They check the chicken houses, and once again, there are human like spoor in the vicinity of the fowls, but no damage done to the wire or bars. It's possible that Bodger disturbed whatever was there, and his charge out of the kitchen interrupted the intruder.

Tonight they'll be ready for any unwelcome nocturnal visit.

***

Night comes around and with it the full moon. David and Adele, along with Bodger have a makeshift camp in the kitchen. David is armed once again with the rifle, while Adele has the 9 mil close at hand. Plenty of coffee on tap, and this time the back door is not locked, in order to allow them the element of surprise. This time there will be no warning of a bolt being drawn back, this time the door will open, and they can confront the intruder.

The safety is off on both the rifle and the pistol. Both sit in chairs facing the door, with Bodger between them. The idea is that as soon as the dog reacts to whatever is there, to open the door, let him out, Adele to shine the torch, and David to shoot the uninvited visitor.

With the moon moving across the sky, the wind comes up and rattles the rafters, more coffee is had in order to stay awake, and Bodger is sound asleep between them. Slowly Adele's eyes closed, she fights the sleep that beckons, while David fights his own fight, both battling to stay awake in order to confront whatever is visiting them, but this is one battle they both lose, sleep claims them, and the night moves on, they awake to the light of day.

The night has passed them by, without incident.

***

Piet arrives with Peggy, much to the delight of Adele, she loves David very much and enjoys Piet's company, but she's starved for the company of another woman, and seeing Peggy is a very welcome sight. The two women settle down with coffee and rusks for breakfast while the men wander off to have a look at the area where they think the intruder left the property, as well as the area around the chicken houses. The dog remains with the two women as he now sees Adele as his pet.

"David, *bliksem*, I don't know man, this whole thing is very strange. It looks as if you have some bloody local coming in here after your chickens because of this spoor, *fok dit lyk net soos ń man sê spoor.*"

"Whatever it was Piet it moves bloody fast, the second I saw that movement, I shot, and it looks like I missed, look there's the bloody bullet hole."

"Ja, Africa is full of mystery my friend, it's a real mystery how the ANC is still in power back at home, shit they are buggering up that country you know, but let's not go there. I have Oom Hennie's reports here from the croc, as well as that poor bliksem Adam, so let's join the girls, and grab a coffee and have a look at what the Oom has to say hey."

The four settle down, and the reports are read. What comes out of the report is that the only trace evidence that the pathologist can come across is as follows: Both bodies had come into contact with a hyena. The bite marks on both the croc and Adam is consistent with the bite of a hyena, and the saliva taken from the bite areas confirms that a hyena fed on both bodies. As to what decimated the body of the croc and Adam, there is no evidence found on either body to point towards the culprit.

Adam's death was caused by decapitation, and judging from the wound area, his head was torn from his shoulders using massive force, although the blood splatter on the panga belongs to the deceased there's no sign of any kind of the blade being used. His death has been ruled as murder by person or persons unknown. I suspect that the possibility of witchcraft is involved, due to the head being placed inside the open chest cavity, as well as the damage that was done to the body of the croc.

Footnote for Piet.

I'm not happy with my findings, so will be making contact with a friend of mine in Pretoria, South Africa, who is also a forensic scientist and send him some samples to see if there's something that I have missed. I will keep you up to date.

The four look at each other after reading through the report, each with their own thoughts. Just what the hell is going on here?

A smile spreads across Peggy's face.

"You know guys, a very good friend of mine, Veronica is HOD in the Department of African Studies, at Rhodes University, and she's written a thesis on African Tribal Customs as well as extensive studies on witchcraft in Africa. She spent nearly five years in Nigeria and Kenya working with the local people there; maybe if I contact her, she might have an idea as to what's going on."

Piet knowing that they have encountered something out of the ordinary is ready for any help they can get.

"Peggy my skat, that's a great idea. Let us know what she says, and if she has any ideas to throw our way. In the meantime David, I have some goodies here that just might help, kom, let's go get these things out of the truck, I'll help you set it up, then done and dusted, you will be prepared for anything."

The "goodies" that Piet had brought along consisted of two flash cameras, each with a sensory monitor that would trigger the flash and record the photo, both would work off a car battery. He also brought three sensory spotlights; these would also work off a car battery. Anything that moved in the area at night would set off the trigger and set the cameras in motion, as well as the lights flooding the area, immediately improving visibility, and allowing David and Adele the chance to see who their unwelcome visitor is. David connects the batteries up, by allowing them to charge whenever the generator was run; it would ensure they wouldn't run flat.

One camera was positioned towards the chicken houses, along with one of the spotlights; the other camera was installed above the kitchen door covering the area directly behind the house, with a spotlight for company, while the third light was positioned so that it would illuminate the area surrounding the rubbish dump. When a photo was taken, a small alarm would alert them to the fact that the sensory system had been triggered.

The system is tried and tested that evening, while the four of them sit around the braai fire, enjoying each other's company, and Piet declares everything to be 100% in working order. Now all they have to do is wait in case their visitor returns, and see what the camera reveals.

Next morning, Piet and Peggy set off back to Lusaka, giving the newlyweds a chance to play house. A couple of days later Piet phones to inform David that Peggy had spoken to her friend Veronica in South Africa, and although intrigued with what Peggy had to say, could not offer any advice until she had something more concrete to work with.

The days and nights pass by without incident.

Chapter 13

A steady soft buzz of the alarm, along with furious barking from Bodger, brings David and Adele out of a deep sleep, instantly awake. The light of the full moon filters through the curtains of the bedroom, giving them enough light to grab the firearms, and head towards the kitchen. Bodger's growls rumble across the kitchen, as he frantically digs at the bottom half of the door to get out and confront whatever's on the other side. His flanks tremble, as he starts another barrage of vicious barking.

David crosses to the window above the sink, and slowly parts the curtains, allowing him a view of the back yard which is now illuminated by all three spotlights, driving back the darkness, and chasing the shadows. His eyes scan the yard, searching, seeking something. The backyard is deserted; the only sound that filters through to the house is the urgent clucking of the chickens, awoken from sleep by the alarm being tripped and the bright spotlights. Bodger's growling stops, but the dog still wants to go outside.

Adele releases the Yale and sliding bolt, raises the 9 mil in readiness, and opens the back door to be greeted by emptiness. Bodger slides past her legs and runs across the yard towards the chickens, his nose to the ground, he backtracks to the backdoor, and then moves off towards the rubbish dump, only to return seconds later, and follow the scent to the base of the security fence in the area that David had shot at a month before.

David steps out of the door, rifle at the ready. He glances down at the area near the door, and there in the dust, he sees the spoor, made by human feet, as clear as day in the light thrown from the overhead spotlight. From the brush beyond the security fence where the light doesn't reach, eyes watch. The visitor turns, a low growl issued from its throat as it moves away, into the darkness, into the African bush.

***

The sun breaks the hold that the night had on the African bush. David already has the roll of film out of the two cameras and is eager to head into Kafue to have whatever's on the film developed. He remembers to replace the film in the cameras, making sure the lens is dust free and ready to roll once more.

Adele insists that she is more than capable of taking care of herself and is not interested in a trip into Kafue. "Besides, we have only ever had any trouble once the moon is up and we have the security fencing, as well as Bodger, so I reckon that I'll be quite safe sweetheart, and besides I'm a better shot than you."

"I don't like leaving you alone here, after what's been happening, but I suppose you're right, once again, anyway I should be back long before nightfall, but keep the mobile phone closes by in case you need to call me."

She watches as David drives out the gate, stops the Land Cruiser, gets out and locks the gate behind him, and in a way, locking her in, safe and sound within the security area. The dust settles as the vehicle drives out of sight, and the sound of its engine fades away, leaving her alone, with Bodger as her only company.

***

David arrives in the town of Kafue and heads to the local chemist to have the film developed. His luck is out as he's advised by the pretty redhead behind the counter. He's told that they can send it to Lusaka, but it will take up to two weeks to get developed, and returned, if he's in a hurry, the best thing would be that he drives through to Lusaka and have it developed there. He checks the time, plenty of that available, only 9.45 am which gives him enough time to drive the further 50 km to Lusaka, find a photo studio that will process the film, and while that's being done give Piet a ring and meet him for a beer or two over lunch, and pick up something sexy for Adele from one of the local shops.

He calls Adele on the cell and tells her of his intentions. "Baby, I should be back long before sunset, time's on my side, and we need to see what's in those photo's, so take care, and look after yourself, I love you."

David arrives in Lusaka just after 11.30 am and heads straight for a studio he had noticed from their last trip to the city. He's informed that the process will take two hours to develop both rolls of film, which leaves him more than enough time to get back to Adele. From there he calls Piet, and the two arrange to meet at a bar across the road from the studio.

Time passes quickly as the two men swap stories, and eager to see what the camera has captured, they cross the street and enter the store. The clerk looks at them as if trying to place their faces until finally she blurts out and asks. "Where are you guys shooting the movie? Geez, that thing in the pictures is enough to give anyone nightmares, I nearly wet myself when the one photo developed, good thing it's only a movie hey."

They both glanced up, lost for a second, and then David realizes that she's talking to them. "That's the effect we're looking for, we're shooting on the other side of the Zambezi, about 110 km from here, please print another copy of this photo for us anyway, Piet we need to check out these prints in a hurry, let's grab a coffee."

Chapter 14

Both men look in horror at the apparition that has been captured on film. Only one photo has a clear picture, but it's enough to turn their blood to ice and send shivers up and down their spines. What looks back at them from the glossy picture is a freak of nature, but then nature would never be so cruel.

It looks as if the gates of hell have been opened, and this is what has walked through. David is the first to react.

"Shit, Adele's at home alone, and it's already 2 pm, I must get back as soon as possible before it gets dark. Piet take this picture to Peggy, ask her to get it to that friend of hers at the university, let's try to find out what we're up against."

"Never in my life have I seen such a thing, man this is sick. Ja you must put *voët my vriend*, and get back home. I'll get this to Peggy, then I'll follow you as soon as I can, you can't spend another night there alone, I must round up a gang of boys to come with me. Fok David, move man, night's coming."

David calls Adele to check up on her. All is quiet at the smallholding and she's sitting outside in the sun reading a novel, supper is ready and she's eager to see what the photos captured.
"Baby, there was something wrong with the cameras or the film, there was nothing on any of the photos. Piet's coming out later to try and fix the problem, see you in a while."

David grinds the gears of the Land Cruiser as he speeds out of Lusaka heading back towards Kafue, his heart pounding in his chest, his mouth as dry as sandpaper, as his mind replays over and over what he saw in the photo. It's impossible he thinks; nothing like that can exist in the real world.

What scares him more than anything else is that this is the real world, and the woman he loves is alone on the smallholding, and he's running out of time before the sun sets, and the full moon once again claims the night sky.

He keeps the speed of the Land Cruiser at 140 km as he hurls towards Adele and what waits for them there. He's brought back to earth with a sudden thud as he realizes that a herd of elephant are busy crossing the road ahead of him, which means he's stuck until they have moved on.

Minutes feel like hours as the great beasts move slowly from the one side into the bush onto the other side, and the sun slowly starts to sink in the sky.

Flooring the accelerator once the roads clear, pushing the Cruiser back up to 140 km, praying that he'll get back to the smallholding before darkness falls. He arrives in Kafue, his shirt sticking to his back, hands shaking and also in need of petrol.

Heading for the first petrol station, the time is now 4.45 pm only to find it closed, and his petrol gauge is sitting just above empty. With a squeal of rubber on tarmac, he slams the Cruiser into gear and heads for the other petrol station.

Relief floods over him when he sees that they are still open, but there are four vehicles ahead of him, so more time is now being lost.

He calls Adele again, his hands trembling. "I'm in Kafue now baby, just getting petrol and should be home in an hour or so, but if it gets dark before I get there, lock yourself in the house."

"David, you're over reacting, I'll be fine, just come home safely."

It is now 5.10 pm and the sun is setting over the African horizon. David leaves Kafue as quickly as he can, as the road surface has started to crumble over the years and not safe for speed, so he's forced to travel between 40 km and 60 km when the surface allows it.

The turnoff is 14 km outside Kafue, and the distance from the turnoff to the smallholding is 16 km. David arrives at the turn off as the sun sets and has to reduce speed due to potholes and rocks all over the surface of the track.

It happens as the full moon rises and only another 6 km to go before he would have reached home; his back left rear tire blows. He stops on the side of the road, leaps out and rushes around to the back to release the spare, he lifts the lid of the spare wheel covering and looks into emptiness, there is no spare, and the moon shines down into the empty space.

Chapter 15

With shaking hands David keys in Adele's cell number. He hears the tone of the ring, over and over, until it switches over to voice mail. He calls Piet next. "Piet, where are you, I've had a fucking blow out, and this bloody car doesn't have a spare, Piet, can you hear me?"

"Ja I hear you, this bloody cell connection sucks. Okay look, I'm on my way, I should be at your place by 8.30, latest 9. Wait inside the vehicle for me David, there are Lion in the area, as well as Elephant, and we don't need any accidents, my man."

David try's calling Adele's cell again, only to once again get voice mail. Now his mind starts to play tricks on him, and he starts to imagine different reasons why she hasn't answered her phone, and none of them are pleasant. Grabbing a pen and paper out of the cubbyhole, he hastily writes a note to Piet, telling him that he has set off for the smallholding, but will stay on the road.

He tucks this under a windscreen wiper and sets off into the already dark night.

He tries Adele's cell again, and this time he hears her sweet voice, and relief washes over him. "Baby, can you hear me?"

"Hello David is that you, I was taking a bath, I can't hear you."

"Adele, I've had a blowout, and you need to lock yourself in the house, Adele are you there?"

Silence on the phone, the connection is broken. Anger and frustration, he wants to crush the phone into the dirt. He starts to run, into the darkness, towards Adele, using the light of the full moon to stay on the road.

He calls her again. "David is that you, stop playing around now?"

"Adele, if you can hear me, lock the doors and keep the rifle with you."

"I must lock the doors, what's that about the rifle, where are you?"

"I had a blowout, about 6 km away, I'm nearly home, keep the rifle with you."

"I hear you, baby, lock the doors, keep the..."

The signals lost once again, but at least he knows she's okay, and his message got through. Once again he heads off towards the smallholding, hoping that he'll arrive in time, but time is not on his side. The full moon looks down on the drama being played out in the African bush, from its post, high in the night sky.

***

Darkness gathers around the house. Adele starts the generator and moves around from room to room, switching on the lights. She's not too concerned about being at home alone at the moment, as the visitor seems to enjoy disrupting their sleep late at night, but she is concerned about David.

She knows he's had a blow out somewhere along the farm road and is on his way home in the dark. She checks the kitchen clock on the wall, it reads just after 8 pm.

Adele moves along the passage to the bedroom, Bodger at her heels, into the bathroom to brush her hair. A noise breaks the silence of the house, but she can't place it. A soft buzz coming from the bedroom and it takes her a couple of seconds to realize that the trigger has been activated. At the same time, the dog streaks out of the bedroom towards the kitchen, with a low growl.

Picking up the rifle, she moves swiftly towards the kitchen, cautious but not scared as the night is still young.

Bodger is now going wild at the door, wanting to be let out, barking himself hoarse. She peers through the kitchen curtains into the back yard but can see anything in the lighted area. Must be a stray baboon or something she tells her self.

She moves to the back door, and unlocks the Yale, then slowly slides the bolt back, grips the handle, and opens the door.
It moves across the yard from behind the outhouse with incredible speed towards her. What she sees, her mind can't comprehend or accept. She fumbles to bring the rifle up.

Bodger flies past her, rushing to meet the charge head on, both issuing vicious growls and they collide. The two bodies twist and turn in the dust as Adele tries to shoot, but holds back for fear of hitting the dog. A howl of pain rips through the night, the rifle goes off, and the intruder runs towards the fence, leaving Bodger lying in the dirt. The intruder turns towards her, snarling... showing killer fangs, she fires again, and in a flash, the intruder is gone into the night.

With her heart thudding painfully in her chest she moves towards the dog, kneeling alongside him, her hand over her mouth, wide eyed, her body shaking, sobbing.

"Oh God, Oh God,"

Over and over again when she realizes that the animal is dead, his throat has been ripped out, and that he has given up his life for hers.

Adele hears the howl carry across the open veldt. With numbing horror, it slowly dawns on her that the sound is coming from the direction of the farm road.

She gathers up the rifle and stumbles back into the kitchen, slamming the door closed and with trembling hands sealing it against the darkness outside.

David pauses in his headlong flight along the farm road as he hears one shot echo across the darkness.

Chapter 16

"Oh my God...Adele."

Another shot goes off, and that galvanizes him into moving even faster along the dirt track towards the farm. In the distance he can see the lights of the house burning, as well as the glare from the spotlights at the back, he stumbles, as he hears the howl, and his cell phone fly's from his hand, into the brush alongside the road.

Adele frantically tries to call David to warn him and to tell him to go back. The phone rings and rings, its face lighting up the grass that covers it on the side of the road, to go unanswered forever, lost and forgotten.

Terror grips her at the thought of David out there, she grabs the flash light, rifle, and snatches the keys off the coffee table and leaves by the front door, unlocks the gate and starts running up the dirt track in the direction of her husband.

Piet stops the Land Rover, and yells "Shut up *julle*." He has just taken the turn onto the farm road when Adele's first shot rings out. He's not sure that he has heard correctly. Killing the engine, and they sit in silence, the second shot echoes across the veldt. "*Nou is daar kak!*" He starts the Land Rover, and throwing caution to the wind, as he hears the howl, he speeds along the dirt track towards the farm.

The other moves down towards the river when the wind carries another scent to it. Its nostrils twitch as it searches for the direction from which it's coming, it knows this scent, it's the man thing from the house, and the scent is coming from the direction beyond the house.

Silently it moves off towards the source of the smell, the moon is full and tonight it must feed.

***

A full moon looks down on the drama being played out below it, David shouts out Adele's name as he rushes headlong towards the smallholding, all thoughts of caution thrown to the wind. Adele hears his voice, full of panic as she moves up the road towards him; she grips the rifle, ready to fire in defense of herself or her husband.

Piet, swearing under his breath, narrowly avoids a collision with the Cruiser stuck in the middle of the track, in his wild ride down the farm road, and pushes the accelerator to the floor. The other, growling, hears the voice and moves off quickly in that direction, blood lust coursing through its veins.

Adele sees a shadow up ahead, moving towards her. "David, it must be David, thank God." David panting and out of breath looks up and sees silhouetted against the lighted house Adele running towards him. Behind David, the light beams of the Land Rover play across the night sky as it speeds towards them.

The bushes on the side of the road part, a blood-curdling growl rocks the silence of the night as the other lunges towards David. David his eyes on Adele fail's to see the rock on the road, and in seconds he's eating dirt and gravel.

Adele sees the other lunge from the bush, and the Land Rover rounds the bend in the road, its headlights capturing the scene before it.

The other had missed its attack on David; he had fallen out of the way of its charge as it had leaped towards him. Illuminated by the headlights, it turns towards David, fangs bared, drool and blood dripping from its powerful jaws, eyes blazing with hunger and hate. David looks up into the gates of hell, helpless on the ground, as it leaps towards its intended victim.

A shot rings out, catching the other, and knocking it off balance as it leaps towards David, it scrambles up, issuing forth a defiant howl, and charges the source of the rifle. Adele stands firm, determined to end this obscenity's existence as it moves rapidly towards her, she fires again, and the beast goes down into the dirt.

Piet brings the Land Rover to a halt where David's lying in the road, jumps out of the Land Rover, rifle in hand and fires into the form that is slowly rising back up onto its feet. Adele fires again, the creature staggers, its growls filling the night and in a flash, it's gone into the bush

Nothing moves the world waits.

Adele rushes up to where the men are. The six guys are now out of the vehicle, forming a protective circle around the three, weapons at the ready. Piet helps David to his feet.

"Adele, thank God you're alright."

He takes Adele in his arms and both sob with relief. "I thought I had lost you, Dave."

He feels tremors running through her body as she sob's against him, the realization of what has just taken place, of what she has seen hits home, and she collapses in his arms.

Piet issues instructions to Andrew and his men, and they start searching the area, looking for a blood spoor as the beast had been hit three times, and they knew it was badly wounded.

They find nothing on the road, there is no evidence of blood on the grass, and it's as if the beast was never there, but the memory of what just happened, and what they saw will forever be burned into their minds.

A blood-curdling howl comes to them from the direction of the house, defiant and unafraid, as if issuing a challenge to them and to the night.

Chapter 17

With a grim look on his face, Piet turns to the two of them. "I'm not a religious man, but something like this can make me a believer. If God made man in his image, what the fucking hell made that, the devil? I saw it hit three times, but there's no blood."

The silence is shattered by Piet's cell phone, making them all jerk. *"Wat die fok?"*

He fumbles with it, and checks to see the caller I.D. "It's Peggy let me take this call."

"Piet, are you there yet, can you hear me?" He hears the urgency in her voice, as well as a tremble of fear. *"Ja skat,* I hear you, I'm with David and Adele." The relief in Peggy's voice is unmistakable. "Thank God, are you guys okay? Listen I scanned that photo to Veronica, and she called me a few minutes ago, you guys have to get out of there, it's not safe to stay there. She didn't say why, but she's flying out here first thing in the morning. What she did tell me is that you must not have any contact with that thing, and don't try shooting it, all you'll do is enrage it even more, just leave the bloody thing alone, and get off that farm, now!" Piet's mind is in a whirl...*Shit, the damage has already been done...*"Okay, *skat,* we just need to pick up a few things and then we'll leave."

The Land Rover slowly moves down the road towards the smallholding. David in the back holding Adele who's sobbing, the recent events very fresh in her mind, how close she came to losing the man that she loves, and the horror that she has witnessed. Andrew and the guides walk ahead of the vehicle, scanning the nearby bush, rifles at the ready.

They reach the house, and horrified gasps come from the guides as the lights of the Land Rover plays over the gates. Impaled on the one support pole of the gate is the head of the dog, its dead eyes staring out into the night.

They move into the yard, where a scene from a horror movie awaits them. The dog's body has been torn apart by something in a violent rage, bits and pieces lie scattered everywhere. The chicken houses have been ripped apart by enormous strength, dead chickens litter the area, and the smell of death hangs in the still night air.

Once again a howl rises from the kopje behind them; the challenge has been issued and accepted.

***

Piet drives the Land Rover to the front of the house, where the front door still stands open, as they were unable to enter via the back as Adele had engaged the sliding bolt.

Andrew and the guides stand guard on the stoop as the three enter the house. They know that the creature is not in the house as the howl had come from the direction of the kopje but still entering cautiously.

Firearms at the ready, and search every room in the house. The cameras and spotlight's switch off and the area around the house are in darkness.

The men outside on the stoop talk nervously amongst themselves, their eyes searching the shadows.

Hurriedly, Adele and David collect things that they need, throw clothes into a suitcase, and in a matter of minutes, they are ready to leave.

***

The attack is sudden, swift and deadly. The creature bursts out of the shadows, onto the stoop, its jaws clamping on the throat of Simon, the man nearest the edge. Blood sprays the area as his head is ripped from his shoulders, rifle fire fills the air, the creature is driven back, snarling out its defiance, hate, and rage mirrored in its eyes, as it slips back into the shadows.

The terrified group is now in the house, everyone on edge, both front and back doors locked against the night and the creature that walks in the night.

Piet takes command and issues orders to the remaining men. They are trapped in the house, and unable to get to the Land Rover without another encounter with the creature.

They have to survive the night before they can leave, and he wonders if any of them will see the sun rise, as for how do you kill something, when blood doesn't run in its veins?

The buzz of the trigger alarm alerts them, the creature is at the back of the house. The spotlights come on, and the cameras click softly as photos are taken.

Chapter 18

A kitchen window shatters, throwing glass all over the floor. The challenge of the howl fills the house, and the trapped group brings their hands to their ears, trying to shut out the sound which threatens to engulf them.

David moves into the kitchen doorway, firing in the direction of the window. There's nothing there. Panic threatens to set in; as they realize that they are trapped in the house. Piet's urgent voice carries towards the kitchen. "David, the generator control switch, where is it, in your bedroom?"

Retreating back down the passage towards the group David meets his friend's worried eyes. "Ja Piet." With that Piet takes control. "*Kom*, all of you, move slowly, we must set up in the bedroom, and stay together. David, we need to kill the generator, reduce the noise so we can hear where this bloody thing is, and just make sure we have the flash lights because we're going to lose the lights as well."

The group moves into the bedroom, they barricade the bedroom door with one wardrobe pushed up against it. The other is used to cover the window that looks out over the front of the property. David pushes the off switch, and they hear the generator slowly start to shut down and the lights dim into darkness. The only window they can't secure is the small en suite window that looks out over the backyard.

They sit, straining to hear any movement. Their nerves stretched taut, each with a prayer on their lips. Not moving, waiting for daylight.

The soft buzz of the alarm alerts them to the fact that the creature is once again in the back. The spotlights come on, the cameras click away, and the light filters into the room from the bathroom window. A thud of something hitting the back door reverberates through the house. The sound of enraged growls washes over them as the door holds; again the door is attacked with more force, over and over until the sound of splintering wood is heard.

The spotlights once again switch off, darkness returns and with it the sound of the creature in the house

Piet moves into the small passage, facing the bedroom door, rifle at the ready. He motions to Andrew to join him, and together they wait. David moves Adele towards the en suite entrance as they can both cover the two men near the door and the doorway itself from there. Both weapons are cocked and ready to fire.

The remaining members of the trapped party remain where they are, on the floor near the bedroom window. Eyes wide with fear, firearms ready, and their hands slick with sweat.

The sound of the creature sniffing on the other side of the door carries to them. A soft growl and then the sound of the door handle being pulled down, the bump of the edge of the door meeting the back of the wardrobe.

As one, all eight of them open fire in the direction of the door, bullets smacking into the wardrobe, tearing through the clothes hanging there, traveling through the door. The creature is driven back by the onslaught of rifle and pistol fire, it's hit, and driven to the floor. Its howl of rage fills the house, and the spotlight comes back on.

It has left the house, and it's once again in the backyard.

The smell of cordite hangs in the air, no one moves.

"Is everyone alright?"

"Ja David, *alles is reg*, but we must get out of here, we can't stay trapped here. As long as those spotlights are on in the back, we know where the bloody thing is, so we need to move as a group and get to the Land Rover so we can get away from here."

"We're taking a big chance, Piet, we need to move that wardrobe, move through the house, and then manage to get into the Land Rover, and still watch out for that creature, but I agree, we need to move, and the gun fire seems to chase it away."

The wardrobe is slowly and carefully moved to one side, inch by inch until there's a gap large enough for them to slip through. Piet moves out first, then Andrew, followed by Adele, with David and the others bringing up the rear. Slowly they move through the house towards the front door.

As they enter the lounge, with the front door beckoning them, the spotlights go out, and they freeze. The creature is on the move again. Has it re-entered the house, or has it moved around for a frontal attack? They bunch together, and strain to hear, eyes locked on the archway between the lounge and passage way, waiting for the space to be filled by that abomination.

Seconds turn to minutes, they are too scared to breathe, the sweat runs in rivers from their bodies, running into their eyes, blurring their vision, frozen in place, listening for any sound in order to place the whereabouts of the creature.

A soft footfall sounds outside the front door, the handle is tried, but the door is locked, low growls reach their ears, soft sounds of movement, and then silence once again.

Chapter 19

Suddenly the spotlights blaze, the creature is at the back. Piet unlocks the door urgently, moves out onto the stoop. Andrew moves to one side to cover the rear, and both Adele and David cover the front as they move steadily towards the sanctuary of the waiting Land Rover.

David opens the rear door and ensures that Adele is the first in. He turns rifle at the ready to cover the rest of the group as they converge on the vehicle. Piet moves around to the driver's side and slides in behind the wheel, hand on the ignition, ready to fire up the motor the second all are safely inside. Andrew moves down from the stoop, walking backward as he continues to cover the rear. He indicates to David to climb aboard once the rest are in. Andrew approaches the front passenger door, which Piet opens from the inside. David slides into the interior of the Land Rover, closes the door softly as Andrew starts climbing into the front cab.

The creature lunges through the open door, issuing a deep growl and buries its fangs deep into the side of Andrew's neck. Dragging him screaming in terror from the relative safety of the Land Rover. His finger tightens involuntarily on the trigger; the shot goes through the roof of the Land Rover. Piet bolts from the cab of the Land Rover, firing his rifle at the creature in an attempt to drive it away from Andrew.

Bula, the youngest guide in the Land Rover panics, throws open the back door on his side of the vehicle and bolts into the darkness, screaming.

The creature lifts its large head to the moon, howls as if in glee, leaves Andrew's body, and turns towards Piet. Bares its fangs at him in defiance and then takes off into the night. Following the direction, the terrified Bula has fled in.

David falls out of the Land Rover, and together, they get Andrew's body into the vehicle, the life blood running from the gaping wound in his throat. Adele leans over and places a towel over the wound in an effort to slow the bleeding. Andrew shudders and dies in Piet's arms.

Piet lifts his head to the heavens and swears vengeance, his large frame shuddering with sobs. Adele comforts him as David fires up the engine, and the Land Rover moves off, away from the horror of the night, the smell of death strong in the air.

They hear the screams of the guide carry across the veldt as the Land Rover moves up the road towards safety. It's as if the creature is playing with him, the same way a cat would play with a mouse. Its howls follow them, almost as if it's mocking them. It has reclaimed the night.

***

They reach the safety of Lusaka just as Peggy calls to check on them the sun rising over the city, starting to warm the day. All of them are shattered by the events that have taken place, each with their own thoughts. Very thankful to still be alive, but unable to believe what they had seen.

She informs Piet that Veronica will be arriving that evening and that she has requested an urgent meeting with the four of them the minute she's on Zambian soil. She's booked into the Taj Pamodzi Hotel and will call Peggy the minute she has checked in.

Piet tells Peggy of Andrews death, which leaves her shattered as she looked at the young man as her own son following the death of his parents in a motor accident.

David drops off the guides before driving to the police station so that a report can be made regarding Andrew's death, Simon and the youngster, Bula. Arrangements need to be made for Andrews's body to go to the state morgue and the bodies of the other two collected from the smallholding.

They arrive at the police station and ask for Sgt Dube. They fill him in on what took place and show him the photo of the creature. The sergeant is quick to recover his composure and stresses to them that this must be kept quiet as the people in the area are very superstitious, and this has all the makings of causing mass hysteria.

Sgt Dube assures them that a team will be sent out to collect the other bodies and to have a look around the area and see if they can find anything that will assist with the case.

Oom Hennie arrives, as he will accompany the team as coroner, they call him over and the photo is shown to him. His reaction is one of absolute horror. Once the old man recovers, he states that the photo answers a lot of unanswered questions regarding a number of bodies that have been found over the years. "Oom Hennie, please keep this under your hat, for now, we don't want to start a witch hunt." "You are right there Sgt Dube, the locals are so superstitious as it is...the last thing they need to know is that such a creature is walking free out there...mass panic is something we do not need."

He turns to Piet, placing a fatherly hand on his shoulder. "Piet my condolences regarding Andrew, he was a fine young man, such a loss my friend." *"Dankie* Oom Hennie...they say only the good die young."

***

Piet takes over the driving again, and drives to the nearest Protea Hotel so that David can arrange a room, Adele can grab a hot bath and try and relax and calm down, while the two of them pay a visit to the second-hand car dealer that sold David the Land Cruiser, as he owes him a spare tire, then go back out to the farm and collect the Land Cruiser.

Peggy takes the day off, and between the two women, fresh clothes are bought, plus all the necessities like toothbrushes and so on, as all that was left behind in their haste to get off the farm and put distance between themselves and the creature

.

Peggy has also offered to make the necessary funeral arrangement for Andrew, once the body is released.

The morning passes without incident, and mid-day finds them all seated on the veranda of the hotel, the men each nursing a beer with the ladies sipping rum and coke. The conversation eventually turns to the events of the night before, and the creature that they had encountered, and barely escaped from with their lives.

The arrival of both Sgt Dube and Oom Hennie interrupts their recounting of what took place the night before.

"Sorry to interrupt Mr. Swart. Hi, Piet, we've just returned from your smallholding, and thought it best that we give you some feedback on what we found."

"Hello Sgt Dube, not a problem, please go ahead, I'm sure nothing further can shock us. Good afternoon to you Oom Hennie."

Oom Hennie nods his head in David's direction as he acknowledges the greeting, but allows Sgt Dube to continue with his report.

"We found Bula's body, about 50 m from your gate, he had been badly mutilated and his head was missing, further on, near your front stoop we came across Simon's remains, his head was also missing. Both heads had been torn from the bodies of the deceased."

"Go on Sergeant, we're all ears."

"On entering your home, the first thing that we noticed was a very unpleasant smell, the creature had spread urine and feces all over your lounge area, on further investigation we entered the main bedroom, the bedroom had been totally trashed, the mattress was in ribbons as if something with a lot of built up rage had attacked it, and on the headboard of the bed we found both heads, their eyes had been removed."

Chapter 20

After the Sergeant had taken his leave, Oom Hennie pulls up a chair to join the group.

"Piet, while the police were busy elsewhere I removed the spools from the cameras, here are the two rolls, I would be very interested to see what these spools hold."

"Oom Hennie, *jy vat ń kans*, but thank you, we'll take these over to the photo studio right away, it only takes about two hours to develop."

"Right Piet, will you please make an extra set for me? "Give me a shout and I'll make a plan to collect them. By the way you lot, the police are treating all the deaths out on the smallholding as witchcraft, as it's quite rife here in Zambia, and a lot of the tribes around here take it very seriously. I'm out of my depth here, but if I can help, I will."

Three hours later, the four of them gather round as David places the photos on the table. He had met the same response from the clerk as before, but this time she wanted to know which American actor was playing the lead, and what the name of the movie was as she loved horror movies.

They study the photos, the attack on Adele, Bodger leaping to her defense, pictures of the fight, then a vast array of the creature moving around the area, breaking down the back door.

"*Wag julle*, go back to that one by the back door, have a good look. Look at the shadow from the spotlight."

They study the photo, and there it is. As clear as day is the shadow thrown from the creature, the only difference is, it's a shadow of a hyena, and yet it's the body of a man.

David glances over at Peggy, "I don't know what we have unleashed, or how we are responsible. But Peggy, I hope to God that your friend, Veronica has some answers because until this has been resolved, I know that I won't sleep easy at night. That thing's hate filled eyes have been burnt into my brain."

***

Later that evening, they met up with Veronica in the foyer of the Taj Pamodzi Hotel. She's a 42-year-old petite red head with sparkling green eyes and a personality that captures all of them in an instant.

After Peggy has made the introductions, Veronica's eager to get down to business and to hear what they have to say as well as inspect all the photographic evidence that they have. David passes the envelope containing the photos over to her; she glances at them silently, and then slips them into her briefcase, looks at the group with serious eyes.

"You guys were extremely lucky to get off that smallholding, because by what Peggy has told me so far, and judging from the one picture she scanned through to me, and what you have here. We're dealing with something that stems from a mixture of witchcraft and black magic and is very powerful, as it feeds on the fear that it invokes in others".

Piet mutters softly. "Ja, not so lucky for Andrew, Bula and Simon, and then there's Adam as well, all four killed by this bloody thing."

She reaches over and puts a reassuring hand on Piet's arm. "Let's start at the beginning, and possibly a bit of history of the area if you know any. If not then I can research it later, as this is going to be very important. Before we start, let me give you a bit of my background, just so you will know that you can trust me in where this is going to take us, that's, if I am right, and I pray to God, that for once I am going to be wrong."

David looks across at her. "Excuse me Veronica, but shouldn't we involve the local police in this and hand over the photos that we have, at least then they'll know what they are dealing with, and we can stay out of this altogether."

"David I'm sorry but the answer is an emphatic no, we can't involve the police in this right now as it will involve too many other people, which unfortunately will mean more deaths. We must do this alone, once we have our facts straight I'll hopefully know how to tackle this head on. One thing that I do know is that you have all survived more than one attack, so as far as this creature is concerned, it's now personal."

Veronica starts to fill the group in on her expertise. She has focused on studying African culture and for the last 16 years, her main focus being on African witchcraft, primarily the area of study that she concentrated on was the use of body parts in traditional medicine, the killings of albinos,' and the myth involving the hyena in witchcraft as well as the mythical African tribe called the Bouda, whom it is said is able to transform themselves into hyenas at will.

During her thesis and studies she has spent considerable time in Kenya, Nigeria, Tanzania, Mozambique, Malawi, Uganda as well as Zambia carrying out her studies, mainly due to the strong belief in witchcraft in these regions, as well as the number of deaths that have taken place in these areas attributed to the hyena through the medium of witchcraft. She also spent a year in Zimbabwe with the Shangaan people who associate the hyena with evil and witchcraft.

Apart from her interest in the superstitions of various tribes that revolve around the hyena, and the use of witchcraft in murders and death, she has also spent a number of years studying the spotted hyena, and is now considered by many to be a leading authority on the animal.

They talk into the night, each with their own account of what they have seen, and it's agreed that a meeting needs to be arranged between Veronica and Oom Hennie so she can get information from him regarding the state of the bodies that he has worked on, as well as his findings, and any other unexplained deaths that have taken place over the years, in order to assist her in her research. Veronica is asked to give the extra set of photos to Oom Hennie when she meets with him tomorrow.

David is asked to visit the local deeds office to obtain information on the smallholding. Piet has volunteered to try and get information from the local tribes found in the area, and if possible arrange a meeting with a local witch doctor. As the belief in witchcraft is widespread in Zambia, and he or she could possibly aid Veronica in her research.

They all agree to meet back at the hotel the next day, for lunch.

Veronica retires to her room, a very worried woman. She has encountered this phenomenon only once before in Malawi's Phalombe plain, to the north of Michesi Mountain, where the victims were decapitated. Five deaths were recorded in 2004, five in 2005 and six in 2006. This pattern continued until 2009 when eight people were killed. All deaths occurred when it was a full moon, and attributed to the spotted hyena, but that never explained the human footprints in the vicinity of all the deaths, and this is the first time she has photographic evidence of what she has suspected all along, but was unable to prove.

A photograph of a man, but the shadow thrown by the light is of a hyena. A shudder runs up her spine at the thought of what lies ahead of them.

Sleep does not come easy, every time she closes her eyes, the vision of the snarling apparition flashes in her mind.

Chapter 21

Veronica wakes from a troubled sleep to the sound of the hustle and bustle of Lusaka, and her thoughts immediately turn to what awaits them, and a shiver runs down her spine. Her cell rings, it's Peggy informing her that Oom Hennie will be more than happy to see her, all she has to do is pop in around 11 am and he'll make sure that he's free. That gives her more than enough time for a hot shower and to get her thoughts together.

David and Adele visit the deeds office and obtain the required information with regards to the smallholding, and Piet puts out feelers amongst his staff regarding the whereabouts of a witch doctor, as well as asking them for any information that they might have, be it rumor or fact regarding any unexplained activity in the Kafue area.

Piet has gone ahead and made arrangements for all of them to travel to the Hippo Safari Lodge which is a three-hour drive from Lusaka. The lodge overlooks the Kafue River and is a lot closer to the area where the smallholding is, he feels that it's better for the group to stay together, rather than spread out all over Lusaka, as more will be achieved.

Each one arrives at the rendezvous, eager to dispense the information that has been collected, and hopefully, they will be able to put this nightmare behind them. No one has slept easily as the images of the creature follows them into their dreams, and they wake with the sound of its howl fading in their minds.

Veronica kicks off the feedback by reporting that she had a very productive morning with Oom Hennie, and shares her information with the others. Firstly there have been a number of unexplained deaths over the last few years dating back to 2008, in and around the area where the smallholding is, each killing had been by decapitation with vicious mutilation of the body. The findings on these deaths are the same as in Malawi for the period 2004 to 2009, where it has been ruled as death by hyena; yet human footprints have been found in abundance at each killing scene

"Although spotted hyenas do prey on humans in modern times, such incidents are rare. According to hyena expert Dr. Hans Kruuk, man-eating spotted hyenas tend to be very large specimens: A pair of man-eating hyenas, responsible for killing 27 people in Mlanje, Malawi in 1962, were weighed at 72 kg (159 lb.) and 77 kg (170 lb.) after being shot, but we all know we are not dealing with your normal spotted hyena, man eater or not, what we are dealing with is far worse."

Veronica looks up at them and then continues.

"Victims of spotted hyenas tend to be women, children, and sick or infirm men: All the victims here have been fit, young men. A news report from the World Wide Fund for Nature 2004 indicates that 35 people were killed by spotted hyenas in a 12 month period in Mozambique along a 20 km stretch of road near the Tanzanian border. Once again human footprints found in the area and the victims decapitated, another area rich in witchcraft and soaked in superstition. The killing stopped, and no culprits were ever brought to book, although the spotted hyena was once again fingered as the killer."

"So people, it seems as if there are more than one of these things in existence, and somehow it has been disturbed, we need to get to the bottom of this before we can stop these killings. And David and Adele can pick up the pieces and carry on with their lives."

David looks down at his notes and gasps. "Veronica you use the word disturbed, and that the killings in this area started in 2008, well this is what I got from the deeds office. My grandfather bought the land in 2005, shortly after the death of my Grandmother, but only started building on the property in 2007, which is more or less when you say the killings started. As far as I know, he moved into the place early in 2008, stayed there for three months, and then moved out, and would never talk about the place. He died in 2011, and that's when I inherited the place by default as his only living relative, he never left it in his will to anyone, now we know why."

"Fuck it, man, this bloody story is bad. I need a double brandy just to settle these nerves of mine."

Piet calls a hovering waiter over and orders another drink and continues when the waiter is out of earshot range. "I spoke to my guys this morning and man, what came out from them scared me. I never knew some of the things they told me. This is modern Africa, shit man and it makes me feel like it's the bloody dark ages, these people are gripped by irrational fear and frenzy, and superstitious belief is all over the bloody place. Driving people to attack and murder in cold blood those that they suspect of using witchcraft, family or community members, it does not matter. But what scares me more is that the local authorities are doing very little to address this vicious phenomenon, so it looks like Veronica was right, don't involve the police, we are on our own."

Silence as each member sits with their thoughts trying to digest what has been brought to the surface by the information that has been collected.

Veronica is the first to break the silence. "We need to spread out our net and find out if there was any witchcraft or a witch doctor that was active in the area that's now affected. Piet, we need to talk to the locals that live along the banks of the Kafue River, they might know something, and right now anything that can help us get to the bottom of this, and maybe give us direction will be a big help. I know what we are up against, but I need background information to put a plan together in order to defeat it. There's still time before the next full moon."

"Excuse me, guys."

All eyes turn to Adele who has been very quiet since surviving the attack at the smallholding, and then watching as the creature attacked her husband, only for it to turn on her again.

"Don't you think that it would be a good idea for us to take Veronica out to the house to have a look around, and get a feel of the place, after all that's where it's all been happening?"

"Great idea Adele, I've been so caught up in what you guys have told me that having a look around completely slipped my mind, it makes a lot of sense. Piet, David when can we leave? I think the sooner the better."

"Sounds like a plan. Tell you what Piet; let's go in both vehicles just in case we have another break down along that road. At least there'll be back up this time."

"Right you guys, but it's getting late, which means we'll only arrive after dark, which is no good. No bloody full moon or not, I would rather arrive there in daylight, so I vote we go out there in the morning. In the meantime, check out of your hotels, I've made a plan so that we can all stay together while we work this problem out, and we can head out there now."

"Piet, you bugger sounds like a plan to me, what do you ladies think?"

"Once again, a great idea, it will give Adele and me a chance to get to know each other. Is Peggy going to join us, Piet?"

"Yes, she's put in for some leave; she's on her way over to join us."

"Piet, just where are you taking us I hope we won't be disappointed?"

"*Nee* man, we are going to be staying at a friend's place, there by the Kafue River, almost directly in line with where you shot that croc, Adele, just on the opposite side of the river, it's about a 3 hr drive from here, David, you know the place I'm talking about, Hippo Safari Lodge."

"That sounds great Piet; it means that interviewing some of the tribes along the river will be easier. It will also be more beneficial to us than working out of Lusaka, as it puts us in the area, but on the safe side of the river. I'm sure that both David and Adele agree with me."

"Sounds brilliant guys, but what about all the overseas clients that normally take up all the accommodation? David's told me how popular that place is."

"Not to worry young lady, it's low season right now, and apart from the five of us, there'll only be a skeleton staff on duty, we'll have the place all to ourselves."

Chapter 22

Hippo Safari Lodge is situated right on the banks of the mighty Kafue River, with direct access to the Kafue National Park. The lodge consists of comfortable en-suite chalets and a luxurious Riverside Villa which also has its private riverside deck, as well as 4 luxury classic safari tents, all overlooking the Kafue River. Piet and his group have been given the use of the Villa, mainly because of its four bedrooms, and will allow the group to stay together while they conduct their research.

The camp is situated almost directly across the river from the area where the smallholding is, and further upstream is an old railway bridge that could be used to get to the other side, although it would not be possible to take a vehicle across. They also have use of the motor launch used for river cruises. This will allow them to cross the river and have direct access to the smallholding from that direction.

Their need to get back to the smallholding is strong, and they have no sooner arrived than they find themselves on the motor launch, heading across the river. Once on the other side, they move up the river bank, through the forest, and exit the brush and bush directly opposite the rubbish dump, they move slowly around the perimeter of the fencing to the gate, which still stands open after their flight to safety.

The windows that face the front of the house have all been broken, the front door has been shattered, carefully they enter the house, to find that the lounge area has been destroyed, tables and chairs in splinters, the couch was torn apart, the same is found in every room of the house. It's as if a hurricane had paid a visit and ripped everything apart. They stand and stare at the wanton destruction of their home, and realize the extent of the creature's, hate and rage. There's nothing to salvage, so they move out into the backyard.

Veronica wanders around the area, eyes everywhere. "No bird life is evident; this is the same as the case in Malawi". All around the area, feces has been smeared on the walls of the house; all three women are disgusted with the smell that lingers in the air.

The chicken houses are totally destroyed, the door to the generator room is still locked, human foot prints cover the yard where the wind has not swept clean.

They move around to the side of the house towards the rubbish dump, and a bright red color catches their eyes. Moving forward they see that it's a Blood Lily, growing next to the rubbish dump, suddenly all three women turn as one, nausea raising its ugly head, as looking at them from near the lily is the decomposed skull of a massive male baboon.

Its eye sockets empty, its mighty fangs snarling forever in death.

***

Back at the lodge, shaken by the destruction that they have seen, they discuss their next move.

"We still have time before the next full moon, to get a plan in place, but we need more information. Right now we don't have anything to work with, apart from what we know through your close encounters with this creature."

Veronica looks at the group, and they can feel the urgency. There will be more deaths under the full moon if they can't stop the creature. Adele clears her throat and speaks up.
"Did you notice anything strange at the rubbish dump guys, apart from that disgusting trophy it left for us to find?"

"What are you talking about Adele"?

"Well, I'm not born and bred here, but one thing I do know is plants and Blood Lilies normally grow near water, what are they doing so far from the river?"

The sound of a vehicle speeding towards the lodge, horn blaring brings all of them out onto the veranda of the villa, leaving the subject of Blood Lilies behind and forgotten.

Oom Hennie pulls up in a cloud of dust and climbs from the cab. "Good Day all, I have just come from the office after doing a bit of research on the witch doctor situation in this area and thought that this write up might help you. I have rewritten it, just covering the areas of interest. I tell you, these people and their superstitions, it's enough to send me up the wall, and this is the 21st century, here. Veronica, you might find this helpful."

"Thank you Oom Hennie, you're a sweetheart."

"Oom Hennie, are you going to join us for coffee?"

"Nee dankie Piet, Some of us work around here hey. I must get back to Lusaka, just keep in touch and let me know what happens."

They all gather around the table. And listen as Veronica reads out what Oom Hennie had delivered. *"In March this year, two elderly people- Phanele Lupiya, 63 and Chakumanika Mwanza, 89- were reportedly axed to death by family members in the Eastern Province of Zambia. They were suspected of practicing witchcraft. Lupiya was killed by her nephew, Lovemore Mwanza, 30. While Mwanza was murdered by his own son, Lemani."*

Veronica looks around at the group and then continues reading the article. *"In a related development, an elderly couple, Jungo Chisola and Matengo Sinkamu were lynched by a mob for engaging in witchcraft practices. According to the report, 'The two were severely beaten and logs were later piled on them before they were set ablaze." Witchcraft was also the reason for the gruesome attack and killing of John Chibuye by his son and nephew. The two suspects are currently at large."*

"Piet, we need to find out if there's anyone who knows of killings in this area and is willing to talk to us, as these killings are recent, but as we can see from this article, it's happening all the time. Most importantly, it must be a killing of a suspected or practicing witch doctor."

The days pass, Piet and David spend a great deal of time going from village to village along the Kafue River asking questions, but no one is prepared to talk to them. The three women spend time on the internet researching as much as they can, searching for anything similar to what they are dealing with, but come up with no new information.

Frustrated, tired and at their wit's end, the group feel as if they're running in place and getting nowhere fast. They are running out of time. Time is the one thing that they do not have much of; the full moon is three days away.

Chapter 23

With the full moon high in the sky, the howl of the creature echo's across the water as it catches the scent of the hated "she thing." It follows the scent, and slowly enters the camp area, moving from shadow to shadow. Stealthily it advances on the villa, the urge to howl out its defiance at the world is strong, but all that is issued from that mighty throat is a low growl. It moves across the veranda towards the front of the villa. The hated scent of the female inside getting stronger. There it finds the sliding door open; it slips inside, the pad of its footsteps hardly breaking the silence.

It sees the hated "she thing", the one who has stood up to it, the one who has shown no fear in the face of death. Now it will pay for the creature will rip out her throat. It springs onto the sleeping form that is Adele.

Adele screams, her arms flailing the air, fighting the demon in her dream. David jerks awake at the sound of the scream, and grabbing her shoulder he shakes her awake.

"Baby, you were having a nightmare, wake up, it's okay."

He feels her body shudder against him, as her sobs fill the room. Piet rushes in the rifle at the ready, followed by Peggy and Veronica, pity mirrored in their eyes as they take in the scene before them.

Adele's put on a brave face, but at night the creature invades her dreams.

***

The sun rises on a new day, the birds sing in the trees and the sound of hippo carry across the water to the group as they sit on the veranda overlooking the river.

Piet has managed to track down a witch doctor that is prepared to talk to them, for the sum of $100.00 back in Lusaka, which means a trip back to the city.

They arrive in Lusaka and drive directly to the house that the witch doctor operates from. On arrival, they are met at the door by an old man, who greets them and invites them inside. He introduces himself as Gumbia and informs them that he has been a witch doctor almost all his life and deals with healing. But he is prepared to talk to them about witchcraft and black magic, as soon as the $100.00 is in his pocket.

They sit in a circle, on a grass mat as Gumbia asks the spirits for guidance. His eyes roll to the top of his head and it's almost as if the old man goes into a trance, sweat breaks out on his forehead, and his whole body starts to shudder, almost as if he's having a fit. His eyes jerk open, and he focuses on Veronica.

"I cannot help you, lady, it is dangerous for what the spirits showed me is far stronger than my medicine. This is evil, and you must all leave this place." He looks at Adele and David. "You are in great danger, you must never return to your home. I am sorry but this magic is too powerful, there is nothing that I can do. Take your money and leave this place."

As they leave, the old man touches Veronica on the shoulder. "There is one thing I can tell you, Madam, remember that the Lilies grow where evil lies. Tread carefully, for this is powerful evil magic at work here. Now you must leave, for your presence here has tainted my home."

Perplexed and disappointed, as well as shaken by the reaction of the witch doctor, as well as what he had to say, the group return to the Lodge, more determined than ever to put an end to it all.

On arrival back at the Lodge, they find a very excited Peggy waiting for them.

***

"Guys, while the four of you were gone, I've been surfing the internet, and have found some really strange stories regarding witchcraft and the hyena. Maybe, just maybe there's a clue buried in it all.

They huddle around the screen of the lap top and scroll through the following: Some of the information they already know from the research conducted so far into witchcraft in Africa, but Peggy's excitement was contagious so they played along.

In Africa, the hyena is associated with witches (much like the cat is in Europe). Many different cultures believe that witches can turn themselves into hyenas.

The Wambugwe (Tanzania) believe that "every witch possesses one or more hyenas which are branded (invisible to normal eyes) with his mark, and to which he refers as his 'night cattle.' Some people say that all hyenas are owned by witches -- that there are no free or wild hyenas. At regular intervals, all witches of the land ride their hyenas to a prearranged place in the forest for a saturnalian gathering, where they boast of their evil deeds and perform obscene rites." (Robert F. Gray, in Witchcraft and Sorcery in East Africa).

Hyenas are supposed to bear their young in a witch's house, and the witch milks the hyena. If you kill a hyena, the witch will kill you through magic. Witches are believed to ride hyenas naked through the night carrying torches they refuel with hyena butter.

Hyenas are commonly associated with death because they are scavengers who eat carrion. The hyena can be a messenger or bringer of death.

Belief in were-hyenas is so entrenched in the Bornu people of Nigeria and that their language contains a specific word, 'bultungin', which translates as 'I change myself into a hyena.'

The Wambugwe people paint a Goys-like picture of a "witch riding naked at full gallop through the night, mounted on a hyena and carrying a flaming torch which he refuels from time to time from a gourd of hyena butter slung over his shoulder."

Although what Peggy has come across is interesting, and shows the use of the hyena in witchcraft, but it does not answer any questions that hang over their heads. What are they dealing with, and how do they destroy it?

Chapter 24

Days pass swiftly by, and frustration sets in, so far they have achieved nothing. No one has been prepared to talk to them, and their investigation is going nowhere fast

That evening, the group gathers in the bar area of the boma for supper and drinks sitting around the fire. As usual the conversation centers around the creature that they have seen, its origin, and how to get rid of it, and as they sit under the stars, next to the fire with the brilliance of the full moon shining down on the river, they hear the haunting howl of the creature as it answers the call of the moon, and they shift nervously in their chairs. Glancing around as the night lays claim to the land.

"Guys, not to worry, we have the river between us man."

"Piet's correct, as far as I know from previous experience that thing is bound on that side, and will not be able to cross over. If I'm correct in my assumption, and if it's what I think it is, it must remain in the area where it died."

"God Veronica, I pray you're right, just look at the moon up there, and as bright as anything and the last thing I need right now is another face to face with that thing."

"Adele, you do realize that we are going to have to confront it eventually."

"I know that David, but hopefully when we do, we'll know what we're up against, and be better prepared."

"Adele's right guys, we all saw that bullets don't kill the bloody thing, they might push it back, but I agree; we are not ready just yet. Hopefully, Veronica, something will give and my guys will come through with some information."

"We need to know of any witch doctor activity in that area. And more importantly of any murders that might have taken place, ja Piet, I pray that something filters through soon, so that I can work out how to tackle this problem head on."

***

The moon climbs slowly into the sky. David throws more wood on the dying fire; sparks flying into the still night air, the flames attack the wood hungrily. And the sound of hippo filters across the water and the group relax as the evening wears on

A figure slowly approaches the Lodge, and carefully slips in, keeping to the shadows so as not to be seen and moves slowly towards the bar area, a staff member leaves the staff camp, and the figure blends in with the shadows.

"Girls, I need to collect something from my room, are you going to keep me company, and give the men folks a chance to have a man to man?"

"Sure Veronica, I could do with a walk, stretch the legs and so on, come along Adele, the moon will light our way."

The figure moves forward towards the sound of the voices, but again freezes in the shadows as the three women leave and head towards the villa, then softly follows them.

Talking together the women enter the villa, unaware of being observed from the nearby brush in the camp. Its eyes alert for any movement, the figure settles down to wait for their return.

The sound of their voices alerts the figure to the return of the women, and it waits for them to come into view.

Adele is the first to hear the rustle in the bush as they walk past. She turns as the figure steps out into their path, Peggy stifles a scream at the sight of the silhouette, and Veronica reaches for the pistol in her carry bag as the figure moves towards them.

***

"Madam, Madam Peggy, it's me, Philip from the safari guides, do not be afraid."

"Damn it, Philip, you scared the holy shit out of us creeping up on us like that."

"I'm sorry for that Madam Peggy, but they must not see me. I must talk with Bwana Piet, I have information for him."

"Alright Philip, wait here, we'll fetch Bwana Piet, and you can talk."

The three move off to the Bar area, and Peggy softly informs Piet about the arrival of Philip, and his need to talk to him. Together they move back to the villa, and the waiting Philip.

"Philip, *wat maak jy hier*? Shit did you walk all the way from Lusaka; this must be very important? Come into the house and talk to me."

"Bwana Piet, I'm afraid, if they see me, they will kill me, but I must tell you what I know. It has been with me since I was a boy, and after many nights and days of fighting with my conscious after you spoke to us, I have asked for guidance from the church and it is clear what I must do. I must tell you what I know."

"Philip, does anyone know that you are here?"

"No Bwana, I left Lusaka the night before full moon, and have stayed off the road to make sure no-one saw me."

Peggy looks at him in disbelief.

"Philip, you've been traveling for two nights, have you eaten or had anything to drink?"

"No Madam, nothing, I had to leave in the dark so I was not seen. What I have to tell Bwana Piet is very important; it is something that I have kept inside me since I was a child."

"Kom Philip, no one will see you here, come into the house."

He looks around the Lodge area, sees no one, and quickly follows them into the sanctuary of the villa. Adele and Peggy put some food together for him, along with a strong cup of coffee, and join the group in the lounge where Philip is talking in a hushed tone. His face betrays him, and they can see that he is scared out of his wits, but because of his loyalty towards Piet, he has put his life in danger and come forward.

The five of them listen to what Philip has to say, no one interrupts him as he goes into great detail regarding the practice of witchcraft in the area. He explains that professional witch doctors and witch finders still exist in Zambia and that they are often consulted and contracted to "treat" or exorcises witchcraft from individuals and communities. He also tells of informal witch hunting gangs that exist in the communities and explains that witch lynching mobs easily spring into action to deliver justice to an alleged witch, if they suspect that witch of black magic or body part muti. The name of these gangs that belong to the witch hunting cult is 'Bamucapi', and they are still active to this day.

Chapter 25

Then Philip drops the bombshell.

"My father is a member of bamucapi. This I have known since a child, but he is too old now to be active. He is a member of the controlling council and I know that he was involved in more than one killing of a witch. Bwana Piet, you need to talk to him, before the afterlife calls him."

Veronica looks at the group gathered around Philip. "This is the break we've been waiting for; finally we just might have the missing pieces to this puzzle." She grips Philips' arm and asks, "Philip, this is very important, you say the afterlife will call him, is your father sick?"

"Yes Madam Veronica, he is old and has malaria and is busy dying, and I do not know when the spirit will take him, you need to talk to him as soon as possible."

"Philip, does your father know that you have come to us?"

"Yes Bwana Piet, the drums have carried the message through the air and he knows of Madam Veronica and the demon that walks at night, and I have his blessing for this. He has converted to the church, and feels the need to confess, but will only confess to the pastor from the church, and has instructed me to say that only Madam Veronica can be there to hear, as she is the one who hunts the demon."

"Shit, he knows about the creature." David looks at the others in shock

"That is correct young master, my father has known about the creature for many years, but only he can tell the story, as it is one thing he has never spoken about, it has haunted his dreams for many seasons now, and this I know after confronting him with what I know."

Adele leans in; the story coming out of Philips' lips has her mesmerized. "Philip, if your father gave you his blessing to come to us, what are you scared of, who will kill you?"

"The Bamucapi will kill me, for they are responsible for many murders in the area, and will be afraid that I will expose them. A lot of innocent people are killed because of the belief in witchcraft, and many of the murders go unsolved."

"Okay Philip, we need to move fast, can you take us to your father?"

"I can do that Bwana Piet, but I can't be seen with you, I will take you to the church, and the Madam can go to him with the white man who is the pastor."

"We understand Philip, and we thank you for the risk that you have taken to get here, it will not be forgotten."

Veronica looks at Philip. "How does your father know about me?"

"Madam Veronica, my father was in Malawi the same time that you were investigating the killing by a hyena, and the memory of your bravery has remained with him all these years, the man you saved from the man eater was my father."

***

The Land Rover and Land Cruiser arrive on the outskirts of Lusaka, just as the sun is starting to crest the horizon, painting the sky a brilliant red. Philip gives them directions to the church then he leaves the safety of the Land Rover and creeps into the shadows.

They find the small church, set back on a large piece of ground, and discover that an early morning service is in progress as the sound of singing fills the air. The group makes their way up the path to the entrance and peer in. Pews are filled with people, so they take up position along the back wall, and wait for the service to come to an end.

Looking up at the new arrivals the pastor's eyes meet with Veronica's across the heads of the early morning worshipers, he smiles knowingly, breaks eye contact and joins in with the singing once more.

When the service comes to an end, the pastor moves down the aisle to the door in order to greet the members of the congregation as they leave, as he passes the group, he turns to Veronica.

"I have been expecting you."

Pastor Steve has been the pastor of the "Holy Wings Church" for over 20 years, where he has worked with and dealt with the people in the community that surrounds the church. He has been there for their weddings, births, deaths, their times of sorrow and of joy, and as a whole the community trust him and look up to him, and this is the reason that Philip's father has agreed to talk to Veronica, not only because of what happened in Malawi all those years ago, but because Pastor Steve has convinced him to, and told him that it was the right thing to do.

Pastor Steve is well aware of the practice of witchcraft in the region and the use of witch doctors as he continues. "The fear of evil spiritual forces hovers like a cloud over African Christianity. Dealing with (and in) witchcraft isn't foreign to the church. In fact, the Yoruba people of southwest Nigeria say, "Olorun ko ko aafo," i.e., "God is not opposed to native remedies." "In times of crisis, even Christians may consult medicine men."

"Come," he says, "The old man does not have long to live, and I believe that he has the answers to your questions, but if we don't hurry, the answers will die with him."

Veronica leaves with him, while the others wait on the steps of the church. They walk down the red dusty road towards an old house sitting in the shade of a massive baobab tree; on the side of the house is a small chicken hock, the sounds of the clucking carries on the still morning air, the sky thick with smoke from cooking fires, as he pushes open the rusted front gate, leading up to the front door.

The pastor knocks and they wait. They hear a shuffling from inside and the door is opened by an old woman. "Good Morning Mama, I have brought the young woman to see Dada, as he requested."

She moves to one side, not saying a word, and allows them to enter the dimly lit house; the smell of death hangs in the air.

Chapter 26

They move down a narrow passage towards the room at the back of the house, a blanket hangs from the empty door frame, cutting the room off from the rest of the world, the pastor pushes it to one side, and they enter the room. The figure lying on the bed shocks Veronica, the eyes are sunken into his skull, the once muscular frame has now been reduced to skin and bone, the man she once knew has been ravaged by age and the sickness and she knows that he hasn't got long to go.

"Dada, the woman is here."

The old man's head turns in the direction of the voice; a skeletal arm moves out from underneath the blanket and reaches out in her direction. Veronica realizes with shock that not only is he dying, but he's blind as well, and gently takes his hand in hers.

"Mossie, it's I, Veronica, I need your help, my old friend, as one who walked in Malawi now walks here." The voice that comes from the old man is still strong and clear.

"It's good to hear your voice; I have lived longer because of you, and I know of the creature that you seek. You saved my life, and because of that I will confess to you and Pastor Steve."

His hand tightens its grip on Veronica's hand; a tremor runs through his body. "It needs to be destroyed, because of me it lives, and it is evil."

A chill runs up Veronica's spine as she sits in rapt attention listening to the old man recount what took place so many years ago, and what has plagued his dreams ever since.

As a young man, he was brought up in a home full of superstition and fear of the unexplained, and at the age of 14 years, he witnessed his first witchcraft killing. He joined the Bamucapi when he turned 16 and took part in many killings of witches, and people believed to be involved in witchcraft, these people were men, women, and children.

She listens in growing horror as it dawns on her that; to those who believe in witchcraft and magic, it's a reason to murder and mutilate the innocent. Mossie struggles to sit up, she helps him get comfortable, the old man continues.

At one stage there was a thriving village near the area where Oubaas Dirk built his house, but years before in 1996, a Shangaan witch doctor arrived in the area. This man was very powerful, and the villagers in the area were afraid of him and believed that he rode on the hyena, yet they went to him for muti.

The villagers also noted an increase in the spotted hyena population in the area and the fear of this man increased. Then early in 1997 the first death occurred in the area, the body was missing fingers, genitals, and ears and hyena had fed on the body, so cause of death was unknown. This continued through 1997 until 1999. A total of 37 people were killed in similar circumstances and body parts were missing. In the case of women, the breasts were removed, along with limbs. Amongst the 37 people killed, the last one to die was the old man's first wife, and this was the last straw. The villagers were convinced that the Shangaan witch doctor was responsible for the deaths and that he was dabbling in body part muti.

A muti murder is particularly brutal, with knives and a machete used to cut and hack off limbs, breasts, and other body parts from the screaming victims, including children. The belief is that the parts from a living victim are far more potent than from a dead one. Many of the victims were beheaded, and the villagers believed that the witch doctor had carefully collected the heads and preserved them as gruesome good luck charms or for use in rituals. Mossie called on the Bamucapi and a mob was formed to confront the witch doctor of his crimes, and to rid the area of his witchcraft.

The old man pauses in his tale, and Veronica helps him sip water from an enamel mug that's next to the bed, Pastor Steve bends his head in silent prayer as the enormity of the confession hits home.

The moon was at its highest point in the sky, full and bright, when the mob, made up of men and woman left the village to make their way towards the hut, near the kopje where the witch doctor conducted his business. They were armed with knives, machetes, and knobkerries. The fear and superstition they felt towards the witch doctor only managed to fan the flames of revenge for those who had lost their lives, and blood lust was in their eyes.

Sounds of the mob making their way across the veldt towards the hut brought the witch doctor out from his hut. The howls of the hyena filled the night. Outside his hut he stood, defiant in the face of the mob, his right hand curled into the mane of a large male hyena he had chained outside the entrance; his eyes flashed hatred as he hurled curses at the mob and the sky, and showed no fear.

The mob, full of superstition and fear, afraid to move forward, gathered below the witch doctor. A huge bank of storm clouds gathered on the horizon, lightning flashed down to earth while the thunder rumbled in the distance.

Suddenly, a rock is thrown from the back of the mob, it strikes the witch doctor on the side of the head, he goes down, and as one the mob is upon him, blood lust winning over fear and superstition. His curses fill the night and then fall silent.

The mob turns on the hyena, unable to run because of the chain, and take out their hatred on the animal. A powerful swing from a razor sharp machete severs its massive head from its shoulders.

The witch doctor lies in the dirt, the moon shines down on his corpse as the mob turns to his hut, and soon the thatch is ablaze, throwing sparks into the night sky and lighting up the area.

A grave is prepared, and the body of the witch doctor dragged towards it.

Mossie gathers himself to continue, looks at Veronica and Pastor Steve, willing them to tell him to stop as the memory is too painful of what happened next, but both remain silent, watching and waiting for the old man to collect his thoughts and carry on.

As they drag the body towards the makeshift grave site, Mossie comes forward carrying the severed head of the hyena. "My brothers and sisters, this man killed our people, he took parts of their bodies to make muti, he took their heads as trophies, so I say we take his head, and his body and bury it with that of his hyena, so they may wonder in the afterlife not knowing if they are man or beast."

With that, he severed the head of the witch doctor from the corpse, picked it up in one hand and moved towards the grave, holding the head of the hyena, and of the witch doctor. He stood at the edge of the grave, and dropped both heads into the open pit, with a curse on his lips. "May you never again walk this earth as a man."

With that, he turned his back on the grave and walked away. The villagers pushed the remains of the witch doctor, and hyena into the pit, stones, and logs was thrown on top of the two bodies, and earth is used to fill the grave in.

The night is filled with the howls of a hyena, almost as if in mourning, as the full moon shines down.

Chapter 27

Mossie shudders at the memories of that night. "It's okay Mossie, rest, for now, we can come back later, and you can carry on. The old man looks up from his death bed, his face drawn but determination shining through. "No Miss Veronica, I must tell you everything now, my time is near, and I cannot go to the afterlife knowing that the demon stills walks, I will never rest in peace."

The years go by and peace returns to the village, the killing of the witch doctor in 2001 fades in memory and life amongst the villagers goes on. Then in 2007, Oubaas Dirk comes to see the chief of the tribe as he wishes to buy some land in the area and wants to get approval from him before he approaches the sellers. The chief grants his approval, the land near the kopje is bought, but Oubaas Dirk only returns to build late in 2009.

"He was a good man, Miss Veronica, as he hired the men from the village to build for him, and paid them well for their work, I was one of those men that helped build the house, and clear the area."

A coughing spasm hits the old man, and his body is racked by a hacking cough, and his eyes roll into his head, he struggles to breathe, and both Veronica and Pastor Steve look on in alarm. Slowly the old man recovers, but his voice is much weaker than before, he is now struggling to talk, but is determined to complete his story to them.

"The house was ready early in 2010, and Oubaas Dirk moved in. Then the killing started again, nine years after the death of the witch doctor, and each body had the head removed the same as when he was alive and living near the village. These killings always happened when the moon was full, and the howl of the hyena filled the night sky."

"Oubaas Dirk stayed for three moons in the house, and then just left, I never saw him again. He left the house without taking any of his things but his Land Rover. When he did not return the chief took his things. The killings continued, at each full moon until the tribe moved away, and my family came to Lusaka, and we heard no more of such deaths until now."

His body stiffens as pain shoots through his body, his breathing has become harsh as he struggles to breathe, and the sweat on his brow glistens in the light. Pastor Steve lays a hand on Veronica's arm. "Veronica, you must leave, this man is dying, and he needs to die with his family by his side, please leave us now."

Mossie looks at Pastor Steve, terror in his eyes, not terror from the thought of dying, but terror at the thought that he has failed in his attempt to tell Veronica everything, he knows how to kill the creature, after all it was his curse that brought it back, and she needs to know.

His fingers tighten on her arm, and he finds the strength to go on.

"Miss Veronica, you must find the grave site, the bones need to be destroyed by fire. The grave is somewhere on the smallholding, Ou Baas Dirk must have somehow disturbed the grave."More coughs rack his frail body, yet his grip on her arm is strong.

"It can only be done when the moon is full, and the creature walks the night, it must be done at the time of the death of the witch doctor when the moon is high in the night sky, God be with you."

Slowly the old man's grip eases on her arm, and his body relaxes his breathing steady and shallow, his eyes closed and they both realize that he's asleep. Slowly they exit the room leaving the dying man at peace for the first time in over nine years.

"God be with you" echo's over and over in Veronica's head as she makes her way back to the waiting group, the enormity of what lies ahead of them makes her shudder and sends a shiver down her spine.

***

"Veronica wait up."

She turns into the narrow street to find Pastor Steve running up the road behind her, out of breath he arrives at her side. "Veronica, I heard everything that Mossie had to say, and I believe that possibly I can be of some help to you, please would you and your friends join me in the Rectory for something to drink so that we can discuss what has transpired."

The group settles down in the lounge of the rectory and allows the pastor to have the floor. The others are not yet aware of what the old man had to share with Veronica but sit in rapt attention as the pastor talks.

"I have been pastor of this church for 20 years now, and am close to retirement but I have had many dealing with the superstitions of the local people, as well as the use of witch craft. In Africa, witch doctors are consulted not only for healing diseases, but also for placing curses on rivals, or removing curses placed by rivals."

The maid enters with a tray piled high with bully beef sandwiches, and a pot of steaming coffee. Piet's eyes light up. "Man that's going to go down well, we have not eaten since last night, Dankie man."

Pastor Steve continues: "Magic or at least the belief in magic is used for personal, political and financial gain, but what I heard today is more than that, it borders on the supernatural."

"Witch-hunting is believed to be a form of exorcism, so if you will permit me, I will keep a bottle of Holy Water that has been blessed on me and when the time is right, and you have opened that grave, before you destroy the remains with fire, I will sprinkle the Holy Water over the bones, oh and don't look so surprised, I intend to be there with you, as I want to see this creature sent back to the depths of hell where it belongs."

The others look at Veronica, she is now the leader, and she has the answers. They wait in anticipation for her to share what she knows, not knowing how afraid she is of what's still to come.

Chapter 28

Adele is the first one to break the silence. "Oh my God, what have we unearthed, what Pandora's box have we opened?" Her sudden question sends the room into a frenzy as questions get thrown at Veronica from all sides. "Hold on guys, hold on please, I'll give you a detailed breakdown of what I have learned as soon as I can get a word in edgeways."

"Pastor Steve, you're more than welcome to join us, I think that with what we're up against, a little bit of help from the team of the Almighty will come in handy."

"Okay guys this is serious, very serious but we have time on our side as there's nothing we can do until the next full moon, tomorrow night is the last full moon of the month, so that rules out any offensive on our part, but it gives us plenty of time to get things ready." Piet smiles and looks at David. "It looks like we are going to war, my friend."

Veronica looks at the people who have become her friends, strangers brought together by a force that they could not begin to imagine, a force that rules the night under a full moon. "The first thing that we need to establish is where the grave site is, that's the easy part, one thing that's clear is that the house was not built on the grave, as this creature only appeared after David's grandfather moved in, which means that he did something to disturb the grave, and we need to find it as soon as possible, so we can put the next plan of action into place."

"That's the easy part you say, bloody hell David's oupa built the chicken houses, the generator room, the bloody long drop, after he moved in, that damn grave could be under any one of those buildings." Piet looks around the room worry written all over his face, his eyes meeting Veronica's...her face reflecting the same concern. "Piet, I know that, but without the grave, our hands are tied."

Veronica then goes into detail of what needs to be done in order to eradicate the creature, and why the grave site is so important. She stresses that the grave can only be opened under a full moon, when the creature is on the prowl, the bones need to be exposed, and destroyed only when the moon is at its highest point in the sky. She tells them that fire is the method that must be used, as fire is viewed as a cleansing agent, and as an extra precaution, Holy Water will be thrown over the bones.

They sit in stunned silence as what she has shared with them sinks in...David stumbles from his chair. "Holy shit! Sorry pastor." Pastor Steve manages a small smile. "That's okay David; I feel the same, so feel free to express yourself." With a tremble in his voice, David asks the question on all their minds. "Man oh man, this stinks, as I understand it, we can only open this grave once this fucking thing is on the loose, hell guys just how much time will we have to dig up the grave, fight this thing off, and be ready to deliver the killing blow at midnight."

"Ja David's right, we'll need a bloody army to keep this thing from us, hey Veronica I really hope you've got a plan because I am too scared to think straight right now."

"Piet, to be honest, I haven't thought past finding the grave, once that has been done, and I hope very soon, then we can work out the details of staying alive long enough to defeat this creature and return it back to where it belongs."

Veronica once again looks at each one in the room, she lets her gaze linger on Peggy, her friend, on Adele and David, the newlyweds, on Piet the love of Peggy's life and finally on Pastor Steve, and wonders who'll still be alive when this is over.

***

Supplies are picked up in Lusaka before heading back out to the lodge. Pastor Steve has asked them to contact him as soon as the grave site has been found, in the meantime he would make arrangements to be away from his parish for a couple of days to coincide with the new full moon.

On arriving back at the lodge, hot and tired, all agree that the rest of the day would be spent just relaxing and going over what they know, and try to formulate a plan that's workable, they would be ready to leave early the next morning, cross the Kafue River in the launch, and begin the search for the grave site.

They hear the howl of the creature carry across the water as it sends out its challenge to the night, and huddle deeper into their beds. Their sleep plagued by dreams that wake them in a sweat, and a scream on their lips.

***

The sun rises to meet the call of the day, Fish eagle soar above the mighty Kafue River, their cry echoes across the wilderness, the surface of the water is calm, like a mirror, with the rays of the sun bouncing off it, back up into the brilliant blue sky.

The group gathers at the motor launch, ready to cross the river, and begin the search for the grave site. Piet and David are both armed with rifles, while Veronica and Adele both have side arms, although they are not expecting any danger as they know the creature only walks the earth during a full moon, the chances of any threat are very slim, but as Piet put it.

"Best to be prepared for anything when in the bush, if you are not, you're in the shit."

The motor launch slowly leaves the lodge quay and moves across the vast expanse of river that separates the lodge from the area where the smallholding is situated.

They can see the unmistakable heads of a pod of hippo, as they ripple the calm water downriver, their grunts carrying across to the launch. On the sand banks further up from the crossing point, crocodiles bask in the warming sun, languid but alert.

Chapter 29

Adele cannot suppress her excitement at her first sighting of Hippo and moves to the stern of the launch to get a better look. The launch slowly chugs into deeper water, breaking the mirror surface as it moves forward.

The surface of the water explodes, as an angry hippo bull launches an unexpected attack on the launch, the prow is lifted into the air by the force of the charge, the group finds themselves flung into the stern, the hippo attacks again, lifting the boat, capsizing it.

They flounder in the water, knowing that they were now in the kingdom of the crocodiles, the image of the large reptiles basking in the sun further up river very fresh on their minds.

The hippo bull breaks the surfaces near them in the water snorts contemptuously, submerges and disappears into the depth of the Kafue. There was no reason for the attack, but for some reason, this lone bull, all 2-tons of him had decided that the launch was an unwelcome visitor and decided to establish his territory, and had attacked them.

With the image of crocodile very fresh in their minds, the group strikes out for the river bank and safety, 100 m away. Further up river, there's a rush of activity as the large reptiles throw themselves into the water, lunch has been served early.

The rifles went into the water when the launch capsized, they are now unarmed except for the side arms that Veronica and Adele have, but they are effectively useless right now.

The river bank looms ahead of them as they swim through the brown muddy water, with the ripples caused by the swimming crocodiles getting nearer.

Adele is the first one to reach the safety of dry land; she pulls herself up and turns around to see where the others are.

Peggy has never been a strong swimmer and is at the back of the group, David arrives next followed closely by Veronica, Peggy is still 40m out, Piet turns to go back and help her, as the snout of a 6 m long croc breaks the surface, 5m behind her.

The croc, drops below the surface of the water, in order to attack from below, Piet shouts out in terror, Adele, David, and Veronica watch in frozen horror as the water churns around Peggy.

The huge body of the lone hippo bull surfaces between the frantic Peggy, and the attacking croc. The hippo lunges at the croc, as Piet grabs Peggy's arm and drags her through the water to safety. The charge of the hippo forces the huge reptile to abandon any thought of an early lunch, and it turns and heads out into deeper water, not in the mood to take on the bull.

The hippo slowly sinks into the water, its eyes just above the surface snorts in their direction, and once again disappears into the depth of the river.

"Fuck it, that was a close call, I have no idea what started that off."

Piet holding Peggy who is shaking and crying after her narrow escape looks over at David, "These animals are aggressive and territorial, and we more than likely drifted into his territory and he decided we were not welcome. You know we were lucky because it's estimated that hippo kill 2,900 people annually, and that was one pissed off hippo."

"How do you explain the behavior we just saw? If it were not for that bloody hippo, Peggy would have been taken by that croc."

"Ja man it was too close for comfort, but why the hippo did what it did, I don't have the answer, but they've been known to interfere with the croc when it has captured something, and on a few occasions, saved the animal, maybe that bull is the joker in the card pack, and luckily for us, decided to play an ace."

The group pull themselves together and assesses the situation that they are in. Both rifles lost to the river, boat capsized, stranded on the wrong side of the river with a 7 km hike ahead of them to the old railway bridge, and another 7 km to the lodge, both side arms wet, and the possibility of lion in the area, not something to look forward to, but there's no other way back. The only bright light was that no one had brought their cell phones along; at least they weren't ruined.

"Guys, if I might make a suggestion, we stick to the river bank, and only move inland when we are forced to, that way, if we do encounter lion, we'll have the river to use as a safety net, and just need to keep an eye out for croc, so we don't end up jumping out of the pan, into the fire."

"Great idea Veronica, we must just try not to make too much noise as we go, and I think we must all find a good size stick, just in case we stumble across something that wants to eat us for lunch."

"Piet, not much a stick will do, but at least it'll give us a sense of security, something to hold on to."

"Veronica, Adele, let's check those side arms of yours, see if they are damaged, and at least if we walk into a pride of lion, we can scare them off with a shot or two."

They set off along the river bank, in the direction of the bridge, moving slowly as parts of the bank are very steep and the river has cut them away and they have to move off into the bush to get around the obstacle. Twice the group has to leave the river bank, as crocs have taken over and are busy sunning themselves.

The bridge comes into view as they wearily make their way towards it, glad that they have almost reached the halfway mark in their trek back to the lodge. The bridge is only a bridge in word only as it has slowly fallen apart over the years, but the party is able to cross without incident, and walk right into a welcoming committee.

One of the lodge staff had witnessed the hippo attack the launch from the staff quarters at the lodge and had alerted the manager on duty. He had put two and two together, knowing that the only way back was across the bridge, he had sent a Land Rover to wait for them and bring them back to the lodge.

Thankfully they climb into the vehicle, one of the staff turns to Piet. "Bwana Piet, look over there, under that thorn tree."

Piet looks and sees the tufts of ears sticking out of the grass, about 30 m from where the vehicle had stopped, a pride of lion lying in the shade. He draws the others attention to the pride, then sits back, and let out a huge sigh, he's had enough excitement for one day and the only thing he is going to tackle next, is an ice cold beer.

Chapter 30

Dawn breaks to find the Land Rover speeding towards Lusaka, both men in the cab of the vehicle suffering from a throbbing hangover, not much conversation going on, as the sound of the motor grinds through their heads. Last night's cold beers had somehow turned into double brandies as the events from the day had slowly sunk in, and relief had taken over. The evening had ended with both men, standing at the water's edge, howling across at the smallholding, until Adele and Peggy had come outside, and shepherded them to bed.

For the first time in weeks, they all slept without dreaming. The men in brandy induced comas and the women exhausted from that day's event.

On arrival in Lusaka, the first business of the day is to replace the rifles that the Kafue River claimed as toll the day before, as well as purchase side arms for everyone in the party.

They spend over three hours with the gunsmith and finally, Piet settles on a 458 Lott, while David feels more at ease with a 416 Rigby. Both rifles are a good choice as both are used and recommended as the rifles of choice when hunting big game. Piet also selects three 9 mil Browning pistols, to bring the complement of side arms up to five in the party. Along with the rifles and pistols, ammunition is also bought.

The clerk looks at them with a smile and asks if they are intending to invade Zimbabwe and depose Mugabe with all the fire power they have just bought. He also confirms with Piet that the firearms are to be added to his safari permit.

David pays for the purchases by dipping into his trust fund, they decide to check in with Pastor Steve and give him a heads up, before heading back to the lodge, their beds that are calling out loudly to them.

On arriving at the church, they find that Pastor Steve is not alone; Philip is there with him, they are deep in conversation. The pastor looks up as they enter the rectory. "Speak of the devil, and he will arrive," he says with a smile and rises to greet the two.

It transpires that old Mossie, Philips father had passed away the night before, and the old man had instructed Philip that he had to join Piet's party.

On his death bed Mossie had asked his son to repay the debt that he owed Veronica, by joining the group and acting as her body guard, as he felt responsible for the birth of the creature, and now the burden had shifted to her shoulders, and because of him, the possibility that she could be killed was very real, and he was not in a hurry to meet her in the afterlife.

Both men are eager for Philip to join them, for they know what's ahead, and as far as they are concerned, the more fire power they have, the better.

***

While they had been in Lusaka replacing the lost firearms, the staff from the lodge had managed to rescue the capsized launch and re-float it. They had repaired the damage done by the hippo, and by the time David, Piet and Philip arrive the launch is once more sea worthy, or in this case river worthy and ready to be used once more, only this time there was one stipulation from the camp manager and that was that a trained guide would pilot the launch when they wanted to cross to the smallholding.

It was agreed that it was a waste of time to cross over to the smallholding in search of the grave site, as most of the day had been lost, and the rifles needed to be sighted, amongst other things so all action was put off until the next day.

Philip was given accommodation in the staff quarters, Piet supplied him with a 303 rifle that he used as a spare when taking tourists out into the bush.

***

That night, they once again gather around the fire in the bar area, the women each sipping a white wine, while the two men sipped at the orange juice, and hoped no one noticed, after all, they had reputations to protect.

The talk turned to what was ahead, and the finding of the grave. Veronica informed them that they had a window period of 28 days before the next full moon, which hopefully gave them enough time to get things in place.

David looks up. "Talking of a window period people, the way I understand it and please correct me if I'm wrong is that in order for us to kill this creature, we can only open up the grave under a full moon, when this thing is going to be on the loose."

"You hit the nail on the head, David."

"Shit, no disrespect Veronica, but how the fucking hell are we going to be able to dig up the damn grave, keep that motherfucker at bay, and be able to perform this ritual when the witching hour comes along, is that not expecting a bit much, I mean look around, do you see a bloody army?"

"Hey David, you know the saying, *ń boer maak ń plan,* well my friend we will make a plan, after all we've got seven heads, *daai ding het net een,* and we all know that two heads are better than one."

"Piet, you can joke now, but we all know that when the time comes, the shit is going to hit the fan, and I for one am not looking forward to it, hell man I don't mind saying it, I'm scared to death of what's ahead of us, and I know for a fact that Adele's just as scared."

"David honey, yes I'm scared, that creature nearly got me twice, and you were also on the menu, and let's not forget Bodger, he gave up his life for me, and then Adam, as well as Piet's nephew, Andrew, as well as Simon and Bula but what really pisses me off is that it has driven us from our home, and I owe that ugly fucker big time."

Veronica looks at them and knows that they have a long and difficult road ahead. "Guys, we're all scared, and being scared is good, it means that we won't make any mistakes that we'll regret later, and together, we will destroy that creature, we will bring it down, and we will let it burn in hell, where it belongs. David, we'll work out our window period, and ensure that our exposure to risk is minimal; after all, we all want to get through this alive."

They talked long into the night, with ideas being thrown around, being dismissed and others being put on the after burner. The biggest question that faced them was how they were going to keep the creature at bay, while they dug up the grave.

There was no way it was going to stand to one side, or even offer to help, they knew without a doubt that the full force of the creature would be thrown at them, and if they were not prepared, someone would die.

Chapter 31

They cross the river early the next morning, and although none of them would admit it out loud, each one scanned the water looking for hippo. They had come loaded for bear, or should I say loaded for anything that they may come up against, Piet had the 458 Lott, David the 416 Rigby and all three women are armed with 9 mil Browning, Philip armed with the 303 rifle. Both men also wore side arms.

The time for taking chances was over now and the group was filled with a grim determination to see this through to the end.

The launch pilot brings the launch in smoothly up against the river bank, and the six of them climb onto dry land and stand to look up at the thick vegetation that surrounds them, and which hides the smallholding from view.

"*Luister boet*, there's no need for you to wait here for us", Piet tells the pilot of the launch. "We have no idea how long we're going to be, so when we're ready, one of us will give you a call on the cell, and you can come back and collect us, oh ja, just make sure the beer is ice cold hey."

The launch moves off across the river, as the six of them make their way through the brush and bush, up towards the smallholding. As they break into the clearing and catch their first glimpse of the house since they last saw it five weeks ago, growing inside the fence a Blood lily in full bloom.

They move around to the front of the house, enter through the open gate and make their way into the backyard, gazing around, not too sure where to start looking for the grave site. The building's look back at them in silence, not willing to share their secrets with anyone, and the haunting bark of the baboon is heard high up in the kopje, followed by the shriek of a leopard who has just missed out on a meal, other than that the area around the house is silent, nothing moves.

As one they spin around towards the sound of a door opening. Weapons at the ready, they watch as the door to the generator room, the lock hanging broken, slowly opens, to reveal a figure standing in the dim light. The figure slowly moves out into the open revealing an old woman. Veronica immediately recognizes her as the old woman who had opened the door for them when they had paid Mossie a visit. Philip recognizes her as his father's second wife.

She slowly shuffles towards them, raises her hand in greeting and collapses onto the ground, her legs giving way beneath her. They rush forward as one to her aid; Philip cradles her head on his lap. "Mama, what brings you here?" Her voice is weak, and she's trembling. Peggy offers her some water, which she gratefully accepts, and slowly the trembling subsides. "Philip, son of my husband, I need to talk to the white people, to the young misses, help me up."

Philip helps her regain her feet, and she leans on her cane to keep her balance. David thinks that she must be close to 85 years old and can't keep quiet. "Mama, how did you get here, and why are you here?" She ignores David's question and moves forward so that she is directly in front of Veronica. She reaches out and touches Veronica's red hair. "Young Misses, I have been waiting here for you since after Mossie was buried, to answer your question young baas, I walked here, for what I have to share with you, is more important than my life, I am old and soon will follow Mossie to the afterlife, but first, I must finish what Mossie started."

***

If anyone had had a pin and dropped it, it would have been heard all over the landscape, as the group stands in stunned silence around the old woman. Slowly their breathing returns to normal. "What does Mama mean; by you must finish what Dada started?"

The old woman lets out a long drawn out sigh, her body sagging as if she carries a heavy weight. "I need to sit in the shade, the sun is hot on my body, and I am tired. I will explain everything, and you will understand."

The group helps her over to the shade thrown by the house, and they settle in the dirt around her, eager to hear what she has to say, Philip eager and impatient. "Mama we are ready to hear you." The old woman looks at the young man, sorrow in her eyes. "Patience son of my husband, all will be revealed, in good time, let an old woman catch her breath, remember the corn does not grow overnight."

The old lady looked around at the group, making sure that she has everyone's attention, and then turns her eyes to Veronica as she speaks. "The night that my second husband spoke of, I was there, I was the one that released the rock, for the witch had taken my first born, from my first marriage many moons ago. I married again but it is something that I never forgot, and it is something that I swore revenge on."

She paused for breath and a sip of water. "I know that you sought audience with Gumbia, the witch doctor, and he made you leave empty handed, but when Mossie died, I went to Gumbia for muti to cleanse the house of my husband's spirit, and he told me that I must make this journey and wait for you, for you will fail in your quest for "your eyes are open, but you do not hear.""

"I was there when they threw the bodies into the pit, I was one of the first to throw rocks down on them, I spat into the grave, and heard my husband's curse, as he dropped the heads of the evil one and the hyena into the darkness of that pit," may you never walk this earth again as a man", and I rejoiced."

Unable to hide the excitement in her voice, Veronica asks the million dollar question. "Mama, do you know where the grave is, can you help us?"

"Yes I know where it is, but young misses I cannot show you, for you have been chosen by the spirits to destroy this demon, and for your juju to be strong, you and your friends must find the grave alone, for if I were to show you, the spirits of the ancestors will desert you in your time of need, and you will fail."

Chapter 32

They look at each other, all of them very aware of how strong superstition is amongst the people of the region, and there's nothing that they could do or say that would convince the old woman to point out the grave site.

"Shit, get handed a million dollars and have it taken away the very next second, I don't get it, she comes all the way out here to tell us that, what's the point?" David rises in frustration, but Adele pulls him back down again. "Mama, my husband means no disrespect to you." The old woman looks into Adele's eyes. "This I know young misses, for he is very much afraid of what he has seen, and I also see that you have the courage of a lion, this will carry both of you, for he can feed off your inner strength."

She sits up as straight as she can. "I came here to make you hear, for your eyes are open, but you do not hear, I will repeat what Gumbia has told me, and you need to hear the words, so listen carefully and do not let them wash away like grains of sand in the rain." They all sit forward; she now has their rapt attention, each one waiting with bated breath. She breathes out slowly; her eyes closed and begin to utter a prayer. "Oh spirits of the ancestors, make the white people hear, what their eyes do see."

She opens her eyes, looks at each one of the group, then focuses on Veronica. "The Lily grows where evil lies, hear my words and heed them well for they are the key to ending the reign of this demon that walks the night under a full moon, the lily grows where evil lies."

Her word ring in their ears, as they take in what she has just said, trying to understand what the old woman is telling them.

"I have done my part, my work here is done, and my time of walking this earth is nearly at an end, and if the ancestors are pleased, may they smile down on you when the moon is full and give you the strength that you will need, the answer will not come to you easily, as your minds are clouded with fear, push the fear to one side and the curtain will open."

She takes hold of Veronica and Philip's hands.

"Young Misses, your heart is true, and you will know what to do when the time comes, Philip, son of my husband, watch over the young misses for you will need her in your time of need." She looks at the other four. "You have the courage, but you will have to dig deep into your souls to find it, stay true to yourselves and you will conquer all fear that hangs like a black cloud over your heads." With that said she turns to Piet. "Bwana Piet, I know you and what I say today must speak to your heart, you must find the wisdom within yourself to finish this task. Madam Peggy, your heart is pure, and a light shines from you, stand firm in the shadow of evil, do not falter."

Stopping to catch her breath, the old woman takes another long drink of water, and then her eyes move to David. "Bwana David, do not let fear rule your heart, for you are more than you think, there is a strength in you that is waiting to awaken." Reaching across she grips Adele's hand in hers...looking deeply into the other woman's eyes. "Madam Adele, you have the courage of a lion, share that courage with the others, you will know when the time is right."

She looks at each one of them in turn, her old rummy eyes boring into them as if seeing their very souls, pleading with them to see the signs and then with a deep sigh turns her attention to Piet. "Now Bwana Piet, I am an old woman, I am finished here, please take me home as my bones are weary, and my body aches. Before I leave, protect Pastor Steve, for his faith is strong, but I see cracks in his armor, and his faith will be tested before the moon leaves the sky."

Veronica calls for the launch, and they make their way down to the river to wait for it to arrive. The old woman's words ringing in her ears, the urgency she feels is strong, they are running out of time, and there is much to do before the next full moon, what are they missing?
They see but they do not hear.

The launch arrives to collect the party and slowly moves off across the river.

Back at the house, the Blood Lily feeds on the sun's rays, undisturbed and unseen, the sun bleached remains of the baboon skull look out across the back yard.

Chapter 33

Clouds move in with a rapid speed, blotting out the sun, and the wind whips the dark waters of the Kafue River into a frenzy; the waves toss the launch from side to side.

The storm comes upon them in a rush of fury, lightning flashing across the sky. The thunder hammering down over their heads deafens them, as the rain engulfs them, and the sky hurls hail at the earth as if in anger.

The day turns to night as the full force of the storm descends down onto the river. The water churning around the launch, the waves from the wind playing a steady beat against the hull. The pilot fights with nature to get the boat safely to the other side. The prow of the launch slams into the rising waves, as it's tossed around like a toy boat in a bath, the deck slick from the falling rain. They find themselves having to hold onto whatever is near, to keep their balance and to stop themselves from going overboard, into the dark murky waters of the river.

As suddenly as the storm hit, a calm descends, and the sun peeks through the clouds as if making sure that it's okay to come out and play again, the wind drops and the silence hangs in the air, broken by an urgent cry from Philip."Mama, my mother where are you?"

The old woman is no longer in the boat; it's as if she was never there. David is the first to break the spell. "Shit, she must have gone overboard during the storm, we need to turn around, and find her."

The launch turns, their eyes scanning the river surface as it heads back in the direction of the smallholding, the water once again calm, the surface as smooth as a mirror.

Philips cries of anguish carry across the water. "Mama, answer me, where are you?" Their eyes hunt the surface as the launch cuts through the water, searching, looking, and hoping that they will find her before it's too late.

"She must have gone over, just after the storm hit, we were in the middle of the river." Piet turns to the pilot. "Move with the current *boetie*, and head back to the middle, I think that's where she might be."

The launch moves back out into the middle of the river; all thought of hippo driven from their minds as they search for the old woman, hoping against hope that they are going to find her alive. Adele cries out, and points. "There, I can see her in the water, there she is."

The others turn in the direction that she's indicating, and the launch moves towards the old woman, holding on grimly to a broken log that had drifted down the river; she's about 200 m from the launch. The launch cuts through the water towards her, as the surface of the water, gives way to the emerging head of a massive croc, it moves towards the old woman. Veronica is the first to see the massive reptile and shouts out a warning.

Piet and David as one, fire their rifles in the direction of the croc, knowing that from that distance it would not kill it, but hoping that the rifle fire will scare it away. The croc slips beneath the surface of the river, only to surface closer to the old woman who is now screaming out in pure terror.

Another head breaks the surface, and the group is quick to realize that there's more than one croc converging on the old woman. The launch races to close the gap, the pilot pushing the throttle all the way in a desperate attempt to reach the old woman before the croc's do. Piet and David are joined by Philip as the men fire into the cluster of croc's gathering around the terrified woman. The gap narrows and they are now within killing range, one croc's hit, it rolls in the murky water, and blood covers the surface. Then the old woman screams, a scream that will stay with them for the rest of their lives.

The old woman is lifted out of the water, and they see the crocs massive jaws clamp around her waist. Then in an instant, the giant reptile pulls her down into the dark depth of the Kafue River. All that is left on the surface of the river is the broken tree log, slowly moving with the current, to whatever destination it's going to be taken to.

The body of the dead croc pops to the surface, only to be reclaimed by one of its own. The silence on the river is broken by the sobs of a man, who has just lost the only family that he had left, Philip lifts his head to the sky, tears of rage and grief run down his face as he shouts out his anguish and his anger to the

African sky, Veronica pulls him close and comforts him in his moment of grief.

Chapter 34

Piet and company gather in the bar area that evening, still in shock at what they had witnessed out on the river, numb at the loss of yet another person connected to the horror that commands the African night under a full moon. Determined to put an end to its reign, determined to return it to the hell from where it comes, the group shake off the shackles of grief and horror that bind them and start to plan how they are going to triumph over the evil that walks the night.

Adele sits forward in her chair, the excitement written all over her face. "Guys I know where the grave site is." Piet puts his drink on the table and turns to the blonde woman, a serious look in his eyes. "Nee Fok Adele, don't play now, this is serious." "I'm serious Piet; it's been there all the time, right under our noses. Think back guys, remember I commented on Blood Lilies growing near water, and yet there's one growing at the rubbish dump in the yard."

"Holy shit, Adele, you're right." Veronica sits forward, her eyes shining in the glow from the fire. "The Lily grows where evil lies, that's where the grave is people, that's why this abomination has been disturbed. The grave was disturbed when the rubbish dump was originally dug, and this creature has been on the loose ever since."

"Right, now we're thinking, and working as a group, we need idea's as to how we're going to be able to open up that grave while that bloody thing is running around, Ja and we need shovels as well as a couple of pick axes to break that ground open, remember the old woman told of rocks and trunks of trees being thrown into the grave, so I'm telling you guys now, it's not going to be easy, in fact, julle, it is going to be fucking hard, no walk in the park here hey, *maar soos julle weet, ń boer maak ń plan*, so don't you worry, it will all come together."

"That's one way of putting it Piet, but Piet's right, we need to come up with a fool proof plan that's going to keep that creature away from us, while the grave is being opened, and remember we'll only have limited time to get this done. The excavation of the grave can only start once the creature is out and about, and we must be ready by midnight to burn the remains."

"Shit Veronica, that's really asking a lot, but there must be some way of containing it, because it will be nearly impossible for us to defend ourselves, and dig at the same time, I mean look at us, there's Piet, Adele, Philip, Peggy, and you and I, not much of an army, yes and the pastor, heck we had better come up with something, or else all hell will break loose, and we'll find ourselves deep in the shit."

"David I'm aware of what we're facing, and the danger that we'll be exposing ourselves to, and although time is of the essence and it's of the utmost importance that we destroy this creature, I will not allow this group to expose themselves to direct danger. We know where the grave is now, and if necessary we will skip the coming full moon, and wait until the next cycle to come around before we move. During that time frame, we can put things in place that will keep this creature at bay as its safe for us to work at the smallholding during daylight. In the meantime put your heads together and let's see if we can formulate a plan that'll work.

Piet looks at Veronica, a smile playing on his lips. "For a lady of few words, you sure make up for it when you're serious hey."Veronica smiles back at Piet. "Oh Piet, will you and David drive into Kafue tomorrow and see if you can pick up some extra shovels and pick axes for us to dig with, and while you're at it, could you also bring 20 liters of petrol as well, so we can burn this bastard back to hell, I'll call Pastor Steve and let him know that we have found the grave. I would like to go back over to the smallholding to have a look around the area and to get an idea of what we can do."

"We can do that Veronica, but bugger the 20 liters; we'll bring back 40 liters, just to make sure we have enough heat to turn the remains to ashes."

Peggy looks over at Piet before she adds. "That's what we can do while the guys are in Kafue and the three of us can check out the area, and take Philip along for protection, in that way we won't waste any precious time. Is that ok with you Philip?"

Philips nods his head still too grief stricken to speak.

"Sounds like a plan people, but after that, we must not split the group, we must combine our strengths in order to defeat this creature, remember that there's strength in numbers, even if it's only seven of us, we must stand united in the face of evil."

Chapter 35

Diesel fumes hang in the air as the launch throws up water in its wake as it crosses over to the smallholding, the dust settles back down on the road behind the departing Land Rover as it sets off for the small town of Kafue.

Silence hangs over the three women, each with their own thoughts as the launch moves through the water; Philip sits in the bow, his eyes scanning the water ahead for any sign of hippo or croc.

The words of his father play over and over in his head "Protect the redheaded woman, my son, protect her with your life."

Carefully they move back up the slope towards the house, break out into the opening, and there in front of them, through the security fence they see the red flame of a Blood Lily growing on the rubbish dump. As the old woman said, they saw but did not hear.

Veronica leads the way into the yard, and as one they cross over to the rubbish dump, and stand, staring down at the grave site, knowing that evil lies just beneath the surface waiting to once again be awakened by the force of the full moon. She tests the ground above the grave and finds that it's as hard as a rock.

She looks up and takes note of the spotlights that are attached to the house, there are three lights, one on the corner of the house where they are now standing, one directly over the back door, and one pointing in the direction of the abandoned chicken houses.

"We will need more lights to be put up; maybe the glare of the lights could keep that beast at bay."

Adele looks around at her. I'm not sure that it'll work Veronica, the thing charged straight at me; into the glare of that light over the kitchen door, but you know that saying, blinded by the light, maybe it'll work."

"We could get the guys to rig up extra lights, just to expel any shadows that the three existing lights will throw, and in that way, not give the creature a chance to sneak up on us." Peggy waits for a response then continues.
"The extra lights will allow us to watch it at all times unless it disappears into the bush, but at least it'll give us a chance of seeing it, if and when it launches an attack."

"Peggy, that makes a lot of sense, we must light up the area as much as possible. Adele, how are the lights run at the moment?"

"They run off car batteries in the house, but the batteries are most probably flat by now as it's been weeks since the generator has run, but that's how they were kept charged."

"Maybe the guys can rig the lights up to the generator, so that they run directly from the generator, and not the batteries, in that way we won't have to worry about flat batteries, we fire up the generator, from inside the house, and the lights come on as soon as that happens, could be a plan, but let's put it to the boys first and see what they think."

Philip calls them over to the chicken houses. "Madam's we could use these buildings as a safe house, you see where the Bwana had put the steel rods, they were damaged enough to allow the demon to get at the fowls, but if extra rods are put in place, it would not be able to reach us in here."

Veronica reaches out and grips the bars, testing them, her eyes running over the damage. "Good point Philip, thank you. That could work, but the biggest problem is the digging up of the grave and the protection of the people at the grave site, and right now I am out of ideas, how about you two ladies." Adele and Peggy exchange glances, "Maybe a fence would help, slow it down."

With a worried look on her face and a shake of her head, Adele turns to the other woman. "No Peggy, that won't work, that security fence over there does little to keep it in or out, I saw it scale that fence like a baboon on the night it killed Bodger."

Veronica looks at them, the determination in her eyes. "We need to talk to your guys and just maybe they'll be able to rig up a fence around the grave site, connect it to the generator, and run a current through it, turning the fence into an electric fence, that could be the answer."

They looked around the yard, looking for inspiration and finding none. The problem hanging over their heads was not just the digging up of the grave. They had to be able to stay under the creatures radar long enough to allow them to get to the grave in order to dig it up. That's when the real problems would start as they would be exposed out in the open, under the gaze of a full moon, and Veronica knew that they would have to contend with the full fury of the demon. When it realized what they were doing, for the last thing it would want, was to be sent back to hell.

Chapter 36

Days pass, and the only reprieve they have is when they attend Andrew's funeral, apart from that the group works in a frenzy to have everything in place before the full moon arrives in the night sky. The chicken houses are re-enforced with steel bars, and the doorway has the addition of a security gate fitted. Extra security lights have been put in place, and as David puts it, they could play night cricket under these lights.

They have erected a fence around the grave site, with all the necessary tools needed including the jerry cans holding petrol on the inside. The fence has the necessary conductors fitted and has been linked directly to the generator, which will run live current through the fence, turning it into a primitive version of electric fencing, which will hopefully keep the creature at bay, until the grave is exposed. All the spotlights are now also connected to the generator, which means the lights and fencing will run off the same point, turning them all on simultaneously.

The control box for the generator has been moved into the chicken houses, as this has been decided as the best place for them to launch their attack from as it looks over the rubbish dump area, and they will be in the right position to see when the creature emerges from the depths of hell.

The plan on paper looks great. Piet will obtain an old mule from one of the surrounding villages. The animal will be tethered out in the bush; about 2 km away, and hopefully, the wind will play its part and bring the scent of the animal to the creature, which in turn will draw the creature away from the area. This will be done in the afternoon, as they will have to be in place before night falls, and be ready when the moon arrives at the party.

They will have to wait until they hear the death cry of the mule before the next part of the plan can be acted on, which is getting into the enclosed area of the grave site. The only drawback to the plan is that one of them has to remain behind in the chicken house to start up the generator. Once the rest are safely on the inside, and that has not yet been decided upon, as each one of the group wants to be in on the kill, so it has been decided that on the eve of the full moon, they will draw straws to determine who stays behind.

On the subject of scent, the group will smear themselves with animal feces to mask the human smell, and hopefully the smell that still lingers around the chicken house will be enough to cover any scent of a human being, and alert the creature to the fact that it's not alone, the hunter has become the hunted.

Once on the inside, under the blazing lights, two of them will start digging, the others will stand to watch with firearms at the ready, and the person in the chicken house will give them covering fire, and also act as an early warning system if and when the creature comes back. The digging will be split by the six of them, with each one digging for short periods so as not to tire too quickly.

Deep down inside, each of them hopes that the power, coming from the generator will be enough to repel the creature and with the grace of God they'll have enough time to expose the corpse before the moon reaches its zenith in the night sky, and destroy it forever.

***

They find that they now have time on their hands, four days before the rising of the full moon. Four days to which they return over and over to the smallholding, repeatedly testing the generator control, making sure that all the spotlights work, ensuring that the current is running through the fencing, making sure that all is in place before they take the plunge into the dark world of superstition, witchcraft and black magic, before they come face to face with the devil himself.

The group returns to the lodge to find Pastor Steve waiting for them, dressed in his clerical robes, clutching a bottle of Holy Water, and a crucifix, all fired up and ready to do battle with evil, in the name of the Lord.

They gather in the bar area, ready for the time ahead. Each one with their own thoughts and fears about what awaits them once the full moon hangs in the sky. One of the staff approaches them and informs Piet that they have managed to collect four bags of wild feces from the surrounding bush, as he had requested.

Over and over again rifles and side arms are checked, the bags holding the ammo are rechecked, and everyone is on tenterhooks waiting for the time of departure to arrive. None of them can eat, and their lunch sits on the table gathering flies. Finally, Piet broaches the subject that has been at the back of everyone's minds, leaning forward he asks the million dollar question. "Pastor, can you fire a rifle?" With a smile in his eyes, the pastor returns the steady gaze of the other man. "Yes Piet, I have had one or two turns with a firearm and I'm quite capable of squeezing a trigger if the situation calls for it, which I am certain this situation will call for, so never fear my friend, I do know which end of a rifle to point."

They fill Pastor Steve in on what they have put in place, and how they expect the plan to work out and what's expected from each one in the party. They once again stress the danger that they are going to be exposed to, and his response is that he has always wanted to be a warrior of the Lord, and this is one chance he will not let slip through his fingers.

The arrangement for later that afternoon is that Piet along with Philip will drive around to the smallholding to make one last test run, as well as take the bags of feces with them, and wait for the others to arrive with the launch. They have convinced the Lodge Manager to allow them the use of the launch without a guide, due to the nature of their business across the river, without telling him too much, but just enough to get his okay.

They have allowed themselves enough time to arrive at the smallholding, get settled into position, smear their bodies and clothing with feces, and await the arrival of the full moon. One more order of business for the day before Piet and Philip leave for the smallholding, a small issue of drawing straws to establish who will remain in the chicken houses and activate the generator when the time is right. Piet has cut seven toothpicks, six the same size, and one in half, these he clutches in his huge hand as he offers each one a straw to draw, which they do, holding their breath, not wanting the short one. Once they had all pulled a straw, they place it on the table in front of them, in front of Pastor Steve lies the short straw.

Chapter 37

Time passes slowly for them as they wait to leave. Piet and Philip have already left for the smallholding in the Land Rover. They have managed to obtain a hunting rifle from the lodge's gun safe for Pastor Steve, and the whole party is now armed. Pastor Steve has been told what's expected of him, and how important his role in the whole operation is.

One thing that is of concern to Veronica is that out of the seven of them, only three of them have seen this creature in the flesh, the others have only seen photos, her included, that does not do it justice, and she's scared of the effect that the actual sighting will have on Peggy, Philip, and the Pastor, will it freeze them, or cause them to run in terror, as her first sighting in Malawi had done to her. She had frozen in place at the horror that had confronted her, and lost the love of her life to the creature before they had managed to vanquish it.

The launch moves into the sandbank, David jumps out, grabbing the rope and attaches it to a large tree. Slowly they move up through the bush until they emerge in the clearing opposite the house, there they see Piet and Philip waiting for them to arrive. Both men are already covered in animal feces, a job that none of them are looking forward to but a necessity under the circumstances.

They move into the yard and look around, taking in the surroundings. Pastor Steve walks over to the fenced in grave site and looks in, then joins David as they prepare their bodies for the work ahead. The women drag a bag into the deserted house, in order to do the same. Piet informs them that they need to strip and cover their naked bodies, and then repeat the process over the clothing that they are wearing, "and ladies he says, don't forget your hair as well."

They all settle in the chicken houses, one test run with the generator is done with Pastor Steve to make sure he knows what to do, and then they wait, with flies for company, attracted to them by the inviting smell that emanates from their bodies.

The day dies slowly as the sun sinks beneath the horizon, and they can hear the braying of the mule carry across the open veldt. It has been agreed that they will not speak, unless it's absolutely necessary until they are in the grave site area, in case they alert the creature. From where they sit, they have a commanding view of the grave site and hope that they will spot it emerge from whatever depth it comes from before it moves off into the bush.

Darkness spreads like a blanket over the land. The silence is deafening as they wait for the moon to come and claim the sky. Time stretches and their nerves are pulled to breaking point, too scared to blink in case the creature sees them. They sit in darkness and silence waiting for the creature to arrive. The moon slowly makes its way through the clouds that dot the sky, and its brilliant light forms shadows on the ground. Shadows that move and dance in the gentle breeze. Blowing directly towards the river, carrying the scent of the mule in the air. Time passes, and the moon hangs in the sky, almost mocking them as they wait in silence.

A growl shatters the stillness around them, and into the moonlight walks a creature that only nightmares are made off. Veronica stiffens as she sees what has invaded the yard, she feels Pastor Steve jerk next to her, and from Peggy comes a gasp of utter disbelief that carries across the space between them and the creature. Philip buries his head in his hands at the sight of it.

Standing in the moon light, looking directly at the chicken houses, seeming to look right at them is a man. A man with the head of a hyena, it growls low in its throat and slowly starts to make its way across the yard towards the chicken houses. Its eyes glowing and it snarls, exposing wicked fangs. The breeze picks up, and the creature halts, lifts its head to the night air, its nostrils flaring. Looks again in the direction of the chicken houses, turns in the direction of the mule, and shatters the night with a howl, before making off into the bush in the direction of the terror stricken cry that fills the night.

They sit in darkness, the silence, waiting for the sound of the kill, the signal to step into a horror that none of them ever imagined in their wildest dreams that they would be a part of. A signal to leave reality behind and to step into an unknown nightmare. Pastors Steve's soft prayer sums it all up. "Oh my God, help us; for we know not what we are up against, this creature is not of this world, it is not your creation."

Chapter 38

With the howl of triumph from the creature followed by the terrified cries of the donkey shattering the night; the group knows that the time of reckoning has arrived. They move swiftly across the yard from the chicken houses towards the fenced off grave site. The make shift gate is opened, and they take up position around the grave.

Sounds of the pick axe's striking the hard soil reverberate in the night air, as they break the silence. The air is cool on their skin, yet sweat runs from their bodies. Frantically they dig the picks rise and fall, exposing more and more of the earth underneath. The moon shining down from above on their labor.

Inside the chicken houses, the darkness is complete, and Pastor Steve sits, eyes scanning the bush, praying he will see the beast in time to activate the generator in the light from the full moon. He runs his hand over the crucifix that now hangs around his neck, his feelings on good and evil resurface as only evil could have given birth to what he saw.

The only sound that he hears originates from the picks and shovels tearing into the soil as the group toil in silence, each with their own thoughts, working in a desperate attempt against time for each one knows that soon, all hell will break loose. Seconds turn into minutes, the ones not digging stand with firearms at the ready, tense, looking out into the lunar light, peering into the darkness, and the moon moves slowly towards its highest point in the sky. In the distance, the cough of a lion carries to them. Pastor Steve, tenses for another sound has reached his ears.

From behind the chicken houses, he hears the stealthy movement of something climbing over the fencing and alighting on the roof above him. His body tenses, all his senses fully awake, as utter fear runs up and down his spine, the time has come, but he must wait until the creature shows itself. Nothing moves, a soft growl is issued, and suddenly a form lands silently on the ground, directly in front of him, the creature has arrived.

In the moonlight Pastor, Steve sees the abomination in clear detail as it lifts its head, and sniffs the air. The smell of the animal feces confusing it, the body is that of a muscular man, but the head is of a large spotted hyena, it turns its head towards him. Its eye's glow through the darkness, its snarls revealing the large canine fangs that fill its mouth. The pastor is frozen in place as if ice is now running through his veins. It turns its head back towards where the group is and howls at the moon as it issues its challenge and charges across the space that separates them.

As the howl breaks the silence, the group is galvanized into action, searching for the creature in the moonlight. Pastor Steve fumbles with the control switch for the generator, his hands shaking badly, his fingers find the button, and he pushes down with a prayer on his lips. With a surge of power the generator kicks in as the creature throws itself against the fence around the grave, gunfire fills the night. The creature howls out its defiance as the electric current surges through the fencing and the shock that it carries, throws the creature back, the spotlight's burst on, the brilliant bright lights blinding everyone and everything in the area.

Time stands still. The group desperately trying to clear their vision in order to see where the creature is. The creature drags itself up from where the current had thrown it, shaking its massive head from side to side, the bright lights dazzling it. Pastor Steve watches as it launches itself towards the shadows near the generator room, seeking the darkness.

The group gathers themselves, their eyes adjusting to the glare of the spotlights, look around searching for the creature. Pastor Steve shouts out to alert them, the rifle at his side forgotten. "The damn thing has gone behind the generator room." As if in answer a shriek of absolute rage and hate comes from that direction. With the woman standing guard, firearms at the ready, Piet and David return to digging, working together but the going is slow, as the ground is filled with rocks and not easy to clear.

The next attack is sudden, the night filled with its cries, it throws itself at the fence separating it from the object of its fury, once again it's thrown back, bullets fly. Hitting the creature and it retreats to the shadows once again. They watch the dark shadows as the digging continues, no one else moves and then a sound comes to their ears, a sound that ignites terror in them. The sound of the generator sputtering and starting to shut down. The lights flicker and start to dim, darkness reclaims the night, the only sound to be heard is Piet muttering under his breath. " Fuck it, I forgot to refill the generator with diesel."

The creature steps out into the full light of the moon, now unafraid as if it realizes that the power that was keeping it at bay has now gone, the night belongs to it. Its eyes glow, filled with hate and menace. Its eyes locked on the object of its intense hate behind the fence. Adele feels the heat from that gaze and watches as it slowly advances towards the group, its eyes boring into her. A savage growl is issued from its throat, killing fangs bared with drool glistening from its jowls.

The horrific vision lifts its head to the night sky and howls out its challenge to the world as a full bright yellow moon looks down on the earth, watching the drama and horror below is played out...slowly it moves towards its zenith in the sky.

Chapter 39

With the howl of the creature ringing in her ears Veronica looks into the pit that they have cleared, and in the torchlight, she can see through the space between two massive rocks. The gleaming bones of a skeleton as it lies in the dirt, they are so near, and now fate has decided to deal them a joker. She steps backward away from the grave that they have opened, and the shouted warning comes too late.

The creature lunges across the clearing lunges through the fence and pulls Veronica bodily through the gaps of the fencing. Piet and David fire in unison, Peggy is frozen in terror at the sight of the beast, as it towers over Veronica. It ignores the rifle fire, the bullets hit their target, push it back, but it advances once more on the woman lying prone in the dust. It picks Veronica up, saliva running down its jaws, looks at her, with hate in its eyes, and once again throws her to the ground. Her head striking the rock hard surface and she slips into unconsciousness.

Slowly the creature advances on her lifeless form. They watch in stunned silent horror, helplessly as the drama unfolds in front of them. Across the clearing the voice of Pastor Steve can be heard, he is praying out loud for strength and guidance.

As the creature reaches down to Veronica, Philip opens the makeshift gate in the fencing, and with a primal scream launches himself at the beast. Armed only with a hunting knife, he attacks with a blind fury, stabbing at the creature and the two bodies go down in the dirt. The beast's growls and Philip's screams of rage fill the night, suddenly cut off as the powerful jaws clamp onto his throat, and rip the life from his body.

An abomination stands in the moon light, hostility blazing from its eyes; Philip's blood running from its massive jaws as it once again turns its attention to the group behind the fence. Veronica forgotten lies behind it in the dirt, consciousness slowly returning. With contempt and loathing, the creature's eyes lock on Adele, the object of its hate as it moves forward towards them.

The sound of the gate at the chicken houses opening causes the beast to pause and turn. In the moonlight Pastor, Steve steps out, into the open, clutched in his hands are the crucifix and bottle of Holy Water. The pastor has found his calling, a warrior for good against evil. He calls out to the group. "I'll hold this creature of darkness at bay, get to the launch as evil cannot cross moving water, get to safety." He steps over Veronica as she lies prone on the ground, and holding the crucifix up high, advances on the beast. The creature moves away from the group behind the fence to confront this new enemy.

It is cautious as this thing is advancing on it, and it can smell no fear coming from the man that now stands before it. The crucifix seems to take on a power of its own and glows in the moonlight. The creature falls back to the pastor's advance, its face a mask of hate. The voice of Pastor Steve fills the night as he recites the Lord's Prayer, driving the creature back, his eyes locked with the beast before him.

Veronica looks around trying to get her bearings, realizes what has happened, sees Pastor Steve advancing on the creature, and slowly drags herself towards the safety of the chicken houses. As the group moves out from the grave area, Piet scans the area looking for Veronica but can't see her anywhere in the shadows. Philip's body lies in a bloody heap, his blood slowly seeping into the dry earth beneath him, they move towards the gate in order to make their escape to the launch.

His eyes carry to the figure of Pastor Steve as he stands before the creature. Holding it back with his faith in the Lord, the crucifix held before him, a weapon of good against evil, a warrior of God bathed in the moonlight. With a silent prayer on his lips Piet slips out behind the other three, once more scanning the area for Veronica, then with a feeling of dread hanging over him, looks back at Pastor Steve, hoping it will not be the last time he sees the man of the cloth.

The four of them move off quickly, leaving Philip's body where it is, with no idea as to where Veronica is, and their trust in the pastor and his faith to hold the creature off.

The creature howls out its resentment as it realizes that something is binding it, and for the first time, it knows what fear is. It's blazing red eyes follow the group as they leave, the object of its overwhelming hate with them, it hears as they make their way through the bush. It turns and snarls its defiance at the pastor, then lunges forward at him. Pastor Steve falters in his prayer, his eyes leave the face of the beast for a second, and he stumbles on an exposed rock, the crucifix slips from his grasp, the holy water falls to the ground, and the spell is broken.

The other's stop in their blind rush through the bush to the safety of the launch as they hear the pastors terrified screams shatter the night, then abruptly cut off...a triumphant howl follows and then the sound of the creature tearing through the bush towards them.

Chapter 40

They stand paralyzed in the dark. The sound of the creatures rush to get to them carrying down the slope as it blunders through the undergrowth. The moonlight reflects off the water below them. So near, yet so far.

David breaks the spell that has fallen over them. " Move, move, that fucking thing wants Adele; let's get the hell out of here." They spill out of the bush, onto the small sandy river bank where the launch is tethered. Piet helps the two women into the launch, while he frantically scans the bush, his rifle at the ready to drive back the beast. David urgently tries to undo the rope, his hands slick with sweat, unable to get a grip on the knot. With growing panic in his voice, David urgently whispers in Piet's direction. "Get into the boat Piet; start the bloody motor, that fucker will be here any minute."

Words are no sooner out his mouth than the bush parts, and the horror steps out into the clearing. With a gut wrenching snarl the creature advances on David. The sound of the launch engine starting stops its advance, it turns towards the source of the sound, and its eyes once more fall on Adele. It moves forward but stops at the river edge as the water laps the edge of the river bank. Piet raises his rifle and fires, the bullets cause the creature to step back, David removes his knife and cuts through the rope, freeing the launch from its anchor, and it slowly starts to drift out into the river.

The creature turns once more towards David, blood, and drools hanging from its powerful jaws; it advances on the terrified man standing before it. A voice cuts through the night, like a hot knife through butter. "Hey motherfucker, you ugly bastard, I'm right here!" The creature swings around, all thought of David driven from its evil mind, as standing on a rock, jutting out into the river is the object of its intense hatred the "she thing." Adele stands in full view of the beast and mocks it in the moonlight.

Piet calls out to David, to move and get into the launch. David looks at his wife in horror, what the hell does she think she is doing. "Adele, get away, that fucking thing wants you." Without taking her eyes off the abomination she shouts out urgently. "I know what I'm doing, trust me, and just get into the fucking boat."

Slowly the creature moves towards Adele, sniffing the air for the scent of fear from the she thing, but there's nothing there. She stands tall on the rocks, defiant in its face. David clambers on board, watching his wife helplessly as the launch's motor dies and the boat starts to drift aimlessly in the current. The creature snarls in blood lust and launches its attack on the she thing as Piet struggles to restart the motor and gain control of the boat. Adele throws herself backward, off the rock into the dark waters of the Kafue.

Once more robbed of the object of its hate and loathing, the monstrosity stands on the sandy bank, the moving water separating it from the 'she thing". It lifts its head and howls out in frustration, and rage, gnashing its powerful jaws it stares out at the swirling waters, then turns and moves back to the smallholding.

Behind its departing figure, Adele swim's back to the river bank, leaves the safety of the river behind her, and stealthy follows the creature.

Veronica hears the howl and knows that she doesn't have much time left. The creature will soon return, and the moon is near to its point in the sky. When she heard the sound of the creature moving through the bush towards the river it had given her an idea as to how far away it was, she had moved out of the chicken houses, gone over to the pastor's body to retrieve the Holy Water, and returned to the grave.

With great effort she has managed to move one of the rocks covering the bones lying beneath it, exposing more of the skeletons, and she can now see that two bodies had been buried there as the skulls of a human and a hyena looked up at her through empty sockets in the moonlight.

She bends down, back to the task of lifting the last rock in order to clear the grave. The strain telling on her body as she fights to bring it up, out of the pit, and roll it to one side. Her grip on the rock slips, and it falls back, she slowly lifts her head above the level of the pit, and looks directly into the rage filled eyes of the creature, as it moves across the yard in the moonlight, towards her.

Veronica looks at the advancing creature in the moonlight, she fumbles for her sidearm, only to realize in horror that it's fallen out of its holster sometime during the night, and effectively, she was now unarmed and totally at the mercy of the demon on two legs.

She watches as it approaches her, its snarls of fury carry across space between them, when the sound of a vehicle engine comes to her, and the Land Rover turns the corner of the house, moving into the back yard.

With its fangs bared the creature turns towards this new threat, Veronica sees Adele behind the wheel, as the vehicle surges forward, driving the creature back, up against the wall of the chicken houses. Trapping the demon between the bumper of the Land Rover, and the wall. The creature screams out in rage, unable to move, its rage fills the night as it fights against the pressure holding it in place.

Chapter 41

Adele scrambles from the cab of the Land Rover and runs over to Veronica. "Thank God you are still alive...come girl we must work quickly, I don't know how long that fucking thing will be kept pinned like that." With the hideous howls of frustration from the beast filling the night and hammering on their ears both women slip back into the pit, and between them they struggle to lift the rock, slowly it starts to rise as the moon shifts closer to the witching hour.

The edge of the pit looms closer as both women strain with the weight, determination written all over their faces as they know that this is the only chance they will get to put an end to this nightmare. Suddenly another pair of hands joins the fight to lift the rock, and they both look up into the determined face of Peggy. As the huge rock rolls free, over the edge the screaming stops, and is replaced by a growl from hell, the creature has freed itself and is advancing on the three women. It attacks the fence in frenzy, pulling one support pole out of the ground rendering their fragile security to nothing, leaving them all exposed to its fury.

All three women are frozen in place, too scared to move as it glares at them. A guttural growl that comes from the side of the generator room makes time stand still. The creature swings around to confront this new threat, and there in the moonlight is a full grown lioness. Her muscles rippling beneath her coat, she moves forward slowly, the hated smell of her sworn enemy, the hyena filling her nostrils. She inches forward, her hind legs drawn up under her, ready to launch her attack, her tail moving from side to side. The creature stares at the intruder, snarls, and moves forward, to confront it age old enemy.

The lioness springs, her full weight of 160 kg taking the creature down, the two creatures roll in the dirt in mortal combat, their growls of fury wash over the three women. Peggy leans down to help, and Veronica and Adele scramble from the pit and as one, they turn to the petrol cans, at the side of the grave. With trembling fingers, the latches are undone, and the smell of petrol fills the air, Veronica remembers the Holy Water and opens the bottle. "May you rest in peace Pastor Steve." She empties the liquid into the pit.

The three women slide the jerry cans of petrol closer to the edge of the pit, the sound of the battle behind them dies and they look around to see the figure from hell, victorious slowly rising from the dirt, the lioness motionless on the ground. Movement from the bush behind them and a welcomed voice cut through the gloom of the night. "*Gooi die fokken* petrol in."

This is followed by a volley of gunfire directed at the creature, the creature is driven back, Veronica and Adele tip the cans over and the petrol flows into the pit, the creature rushes forward, heedless of the bullets hitting it, Adele sees it coming and moves to one side, in order to draw it away from Veronica, Peggy moves in the opposite direction.

Veronica fumbles with the matches in her hand, the moon reaches its zenith in the sky, the creature screams in rage and hurls itself at Adele, she goes down under the full weight of its charge,

David breaks from cover and rushes at the beast, throwing himself onto the back of the creature, his arms wrapping around its throat, keeping the massive jaws away from Adele's throat.

The match flames and Veronica tosses it into the depth of the pit, the air ignites in a fireball of flame, Piet's body drives her to the ground as the explosion rips the night apart, flames licking over them, the creature howls out in terror and anguish, it stands under the full moon, its massive head raised to the sky. The heat in the pit is intense as the fire consumes the bones that have become brittle with age; slowly they crumble from the heat, and turn to dust.

David helps Adele to her feet; Peggy joins Piet and together they help Veronica up. They look around in stunned silence, disbelief on their faces, the creature has gone, and where it had stood is a burnt patch of earth, still smoldering from the heat that had been generated. What had once walked the night has been sent back to hell. The gate is now closed.

Relief washes over them, and they collapse in a heap, they tremble at how close they had all come to being killed and at the same time they mourn the ones that gave up their lives so that they would triumph. The group stumbles down through the bush, and board the launch. Piet starts the motor, this time mindful of the choke ensuring that the engine doesn't flood again, They head off across the mighty Kafue River, back to reality and the Lodge.

The full moon lights their way.

Epilogue

Three months later.

Bright and full, the moon rises above the horizon, throwing its beams down on the African veldt, it's lunar light pushing back the shadows that surround the house. David and Adele sit on the front stoop, watching the progress of the moon as it travels across the night sky.

The song of a night bird fills the air, and a family of warthogs moves across the front of the smallholding into nearby brush, wildlife has returned to the area, and for the first time since they have returned to their new home, they feel really safe.

Moon beams play amongst the trees as they shine down, throwing a gentle light onto the African soil, and in the lunar light of the moon, standing strong and firm, a Blood Lily opens its petals to the night sky.

Printed in Great
Britain
by Amazon

32254836R00111